GREAT SONG

The Life and Teachings of Joe Miller

GREAT SONG

The Life and Teachings of Joe Miller

Edited with an Introduction by
Richard Power

Foreword by
Coleman Barks

ISBN 0-9618916-8-8

· M A Y P O P

Maypop
196 Westview Drive
Athens, Georgia 30606
1-800-682-8637

Contents

The Tiger's Nest
     Foreword by Coleman Barks *9*

Burning the Furniture
     An Introduction to the Life and Teachings of Joe Miller *12*

     Rambling At Ease *14*
     Growing Geometrically *16*
     Burning All the Furniture *17*
     Mount Arunachala *18*
     A Sufi is a Sufi if He is a Sufi *19*
     No Religion Higher Than Truth,
          No Power Greater Than Love *22*
     Demonstrating Mahamudra *23*
     Futsacutsas of the Kammistram *25*
     Out and Back. A Draft! *29*
     Warning *30*

Part One: Falling Awake *35*

     Words Stand in the Way of Understanding *37*
     Marriage, Sex, and the Gentle In-Drawn Breath *38*
     Anger *41*
     Practices *42*
     Attachment *43*
     Troubles *44*
     Sahaja Samadhi, Nirva-Kalpa Samadhi, and Drugs *46*
     Sexuality *47*
     Waking, Dreaming, and Deep Sleep *49*
     It's Fun Being Nobody *51*
     Love and Desire *52*
     Evolution *53*

The River Meditation *54*
The Six Rules of Tilopa *56*
Just 10% *59*
The *Bhakti* Path *60*
Teachers *62*
The Spiritual Hierarchy *65*
Jesus and Muhammed *66*
The Real I *68*
Life, the Great Opera *71*
Spring *73*
The Mind in the Head Is Just an Outpost *75*
We're Not Pushing Any Religion *76*
Earthquake! *77*
Be Who You Are *79*
Thus Spake Ramana *81*
The Biggest Problem We Have in the World *84*
Theosophy *86*
What Do You Want Out of Life? *89*
This Too Shall Pass *90*
If Anyone Comes to You for Help *91*
You Don't Need to Worry
     About the Coming of the New Age *92*
Nothing *93*
Savoir-Faire *97*
Love, the Breath, and Just One Person to Another *102*
The Spiritual Teachings of Ramana Maharshi *108*
The Sutra of Hui-Neng *117*
Sufis Are Seed *125*
She Is the Creator *126*
Sufism *128*
Visiting the Dead (Return of Joe Miller) *132*
Broadcast from the Trees (Joe's Last Rap) *135*

**Part Two: Rolling the Wonder Bread Truck
and Other Amazements** *141*

Editor's Note:
What Joe Saw from the Outhouse *143*
Forty Below Zero *145*
Mom and Dad *145*
I Found Out I Could Sing *147*
Psychic Experiences *148*
Wonder Bread *150*
No Creed and No Doctrine *152*
Sandalwood on Lake Minnetonka *153*
First Ray Invocation *154*
Of Worldly Jewels and Riches *155*
Ruby Magenta (The Earliest I Remember . . .) *157*
The Clauvilux and the Luxatone *158*
My Worst Christmas *161*
Before the Eyes Can See *161*
You're There Now, Stay There! *164*

Part Three: Great Liberation *171*

Editor's Note *173*
Some Remarks on *The Great Liberation* *175*
Excerpts from *The Great Liberation*
with Joe's Commentary *179*

Notes *203*

Bibliography *229*

Photo Credits *235*

The Tiger's Nest

Joe Miller is a homemade American mystic, of purest ray serene, *e pluribus unum*. From the many ways of vaudeville, India, Tibet, Sufism, Christianity, and Wonder Bread, he concocted one that burned through to the presence where we all connect, and he lived there with great passion.

In the work I do with the poetry of Jelaluddin Rumi I try to find fresh phrasings for ineffable experiences. Sometimes I get deathly tired of the terms I have been shuffling and re-dealing for sixteen years: love, joy, union, majesty, the one who teaches, compassion, infinity, splendor, deep intelligence, life, ocean, generosity, beauty, emptiness, fullness, practices, and presence. And let's not forget soul, spirit, energy, courage, truth, and those unspeakable cliches—being, consciousness, bliss. I just get flat out tired of *words*, and one thing I love about Joe Miller is how he was always bone-weary of spiritual language. That's why he yelled. FIRE! HEART! LIVE IT FROM THERE! He got stuck on those pretty bad. Words weren't his thing. But rather what two people felt for each other, the surge in the eyes and the chest. Words were friendly, kind noises to make while the other went on, the vibration. This book is Joe's whoop and hollering to help us remember that we're all WILD-ASSED SPARKS OF THE INFINITE!

When I first met Joe, we were talking along, and I said, "Here, let me read you something." A piece of Rumi's *Mathnawi* that I'd been working on, the story where someone on *hajj*, the pilgrimage to Mecca, goes through the Sufi master Bestami's town and Bestami says, "Why go all that way? You can just circumambulate me seven times and be done with it!" That made Joe start singing, and I sang him some old Appalachian hymns, and that was it. Joe liked to talk about *Headquarters*, or the natural state; he had many names for IT, the place where love and knowing mingle. There is a deep intimacy that our truest spontaneity springs from. In another Rumi story a young man very skilled at archery is given directions on how to find a treasure. It involves using his bow and arrow and then digging where it lands. He fires off many shots with beautiful arcs and digs and digs. No luck. Finally he prays and in his prayer he hears a voice from inside himself. "You were told to put an arrow in the bow, but you were not told to pull it back! Let it fall wherever you're standing. What is of most value, and what you most want, is closer than you know. It's nearer than the big vein in your neck!" Right there where he spoke and sang from was Joe's headquarters. Ours is our own to locate and be, as we let the thinking-effort-arrow fall and begin to dig where we already are.

I went a long way once, to Bhutan, and hiked up eight thousand feet to the Taksang monastery, constructed in the 17th century while John Milton, elsewhere, was writing *Paradise Lost* and *Paradise Regained*. Taksang was built around a cliffside cave where Padma Sambhava meditated on his way bringing Buddhism from India to Tibet. The story is, he flew there on a flying tiger. Some of us climbed down into "the tiger's nest," which is a large, rocky hole there inside the monastery. So it was pretty holy in that place, and I tried to get quiet and appropriately empty. I stayed behind, away from the group I was with, alone in one of the shrine rooms where there was a large painted tiger to look at. As I was sitting there, one of the three young boys who were in training to be monks came in, looked at me, went over to the tiger and pulled loose its detachable tongue and took it around to the other end and held it to make it serve for a pink tiger penis. He greatly enjoyed the language-less sight-gag, and I did too. He put the tongue back in its less hilarious place, and I went on with being a tourist.

Joe used to tell a Padma Sambhava crow story. This crow is sitting by a pond, but he has a thirst for some other water, he's not sure what kind. He sets out and flies all over looking for the right water, and ends up at his old pond. There is a wonderful, nearly miraculous spring at the top of Taksang mountain, and the taste of that water is fine, after the five-hour climb, mighty fine. I wouldn't want to keep anyone from trying it. The water here in Georgia is good too. Joe-Padmasambhava also used to tell about the guy who kept tracking the elephant, carefully following prints, after the elephant had been found! Here's the other Rumi story Joe mentioned that afternoon we sat and sang (satsang!) in his San Francisco tiger's nest, about the Hindu elephant.

Elephant in the Dark

Some Hindus have an elephant to show.
No one here has ever seen an elephant.
They bring it at night to a dark room.

One by one, we go in the dark and come out
saying how we experience the animal.

One of us happens to touch the trunk.
"A water-pipe kind of creature."

Another, the ear. "A very strong, always moving
back and forth, fan-animal."

Another, the leg. "I find it still,
like a column on a temple."

Another touches the curved back.
"A leathery throne."

Another, the cleverest, feels the tusk.
"A rounded sword made of porcelain."
He's proud of his description.

Each of us touches one place
and understands the whole in that way.

The palm and the fingers feeling in the dark are
how the senses explore the reality of the elephant..

If each of us held a candle there,
and if we went in together,
we could see it.

—Rumi, *Mathnawi*, III, 1259-1269.

There are many names given to wisdom. In the middle, where the elephant stands, is "the essence of vacuity of mind," Padma Sambhava's "common intelligence," what we have together with our candles lit. Joe Miller liked to call it **common sense**. To feel connected with each other, and with the JUICE that flows through existence, was Joe's great joy.

Coleman Barks
March 20, 1993

Burning the Furniture

An Introduction to the Life and Teachings of Joe Miller

"It can't be taught," Joe said. "It has to be caught." It is the great awakening, that brush with the infinite from which a human returns transformed. And Joe didn't teach, he threw. Around him, you didn't learn, you tried to catch. But you couldn't catch what he threw; that just hit you, knocked you backward and rolled off. What you caught rose up from inside as you fell from the impact.

Joe was an authentic American revolutionary of the spirit. He challenged his young friends to issue their own declarations of independence from the empire of fear and wanting. Joe wanted people to seek the truth for themselves within themselves. He felt that each person had an inalienable right to *life, liberty, and the pursuit of happiness.* Life—as in "the resurrection and the life;" liberty—as in spiritual liberty from the tyranny of opposites; and the pursuit of happiness—as in the inner contentment that flows unceasingly from the depth of the heart if you "let go and let God."

Joe didn't have a university degree. He had no formal education beyond the eighth grade. He held no hierarchical position in any religious organization. Joe didn't publish any books or write any articles for prestigious reviews. He didn't travel the national lecture circuit. Joe had no videos to market, and he didn't organize seminars.

Joe didn't take any money for public speaking or private consoling. He spoke for free, and he would talk to anyone who was interested. He simply discoursed on the dharma (or gospel) as he understood it, and in his own vernacular, the language of the common man with a generous helping of show business slang for enriched flavor.

Joe absolutely refused the role of guru or spiritual teacher. He did not initiate disciples. He referred to himself as "just a friend."

Joe Miller's talks offer a unique expression of some essential human truths. His style was definitively American, but his message was timeless and universal. He had only one subject-matter—spiritual realization—the means through which to experience it as well as its practical application in daily life.

In collaboration with his wife, Guin, Joe tirelessly extolled the way of unconditional love and simple awareness. Joe and Guin studied the eastern teachings without ever visiting India, Tibet, or the Holy Land. They came to their own personal understandings of life's source, substance, and goal by using common sense, a sense of humor, and the love of the Reality. Together, they reached many hundreds of young people both on their weekly walk through Golden Gate Park, and at meetings of the San Francisco Theosophical Society.

Their message was simple—universal love and the unity of life—the essence of all the world's great mystical teachings. What was remarkable was their medium—they actually lived it, they didn't work toward universal love and the unity of life, they worked from them.

Throughout Joe's talks, you will hear a few exhortations over and over again. That's just Joe "beating on skulls," and "shaking cages."

Be still, be very still!

Just BE!

Truth can't be bought or sold.

You've got to do it for you. No one else can do it for you!

You are, and all you have to do is be.

Take a gentle in-drawn breath into the heart, and feel unselfish love flowing out.

Joe reiterated these simple statements incessantly to drive home the message that spiritual truth and power are accessible to you from moment to moment. "All you have to do," Joe declared, "is BE!" He wanted everyone to know that this reality could be experienced without "shelling out any loot" or "bowing to anybody" or "giving up sex" or "contemplating your navel until it gets as big as a washtub." When unconditional love flowing from the depth of the Heart floods the personality, everyday existence is transformed into a communion with the divine. Sincerity of intent and willingness to surrender to what is are all that the reality requires of you.

Rambling At Ease

Shortly after I moved to San Francisco, in 1977, a friend of mine said, "You should meet Joe Miller. He's a retired vaudeville and burlesque entertainer. He takes a walk with his wife in the park every Thursday morning. That's where you'll find him. He's kind of a Zen Master. And he was a friend of Sam Lewis (the American Sufi Murshid) too. They played pinochle together." So, at 11 A.M. on Thursday morning, near the Hall of Flowers in Golden Gate Park, I met Joe Miller.

When I first saw him, Joe was standing in a great splash of sunlight. He was a small, white-haired old man with a goatee, a red nose and brilliant sky-blue eyes. He wore an olive army jacket, blue jeans, hiking boots, a work shirt, and a beret. He wore a silver cross with an amethyst around his neck. He wore several rings (amethyst, carnelian and gold). In a brown paper bag, he carried a loaf of Wonder Bread for the ducks and some of his brother-in-law's breakfast cake for the people.

There were a dozen or so young people standing around, waiting for him. I watched as he greeted them, one by one, with an embrace. He was deeply absorbed with each person, in turn. Some got small talk, others a wise crack, others silence and a probing glance. When he got to me, he looked up and seemed startled. I felt startled that he was startled. He just said, "Oh, you've been here before," and hugged me.

I watched him throughout the rest of the walk, I listened and drank in what I could. Joe rambled at ease, working the crowd, using his show business flair for timing, seasoning his exposition with schmaltz, drawing others into the act, rubbing the bellies of the ego-alligators and imbuing the faint-hearted with courage. Joe and Guin just strolled through the natural beauties of the park, stopping occasionally so Joe could lean up against a tree or sit down on a bench to give a "rap" on the twists and turns of life on the Path. Afterward, he would call on some young friend to lead a Sufi practice or sing a ballad or perform an improvisational dance.

"I see you watching the old man," he laughed later, "taking it all in." A barrier collapsed inside, a dam burst, an irreversible change reaction began. Silently, I vowed for my own sake, to stay around him and *take it all in.*

Joe wasn't interested in little sheep, bah, bah, bah. Unless, of course, they were black sheep. He wanted "goats and giraffes." Goats are stubborn, they kick, they eat everything and they can climb high up where others can't. Giraffes are rather unusual looking creatures. They can reach far above the heads of all the other animals and they can't help but stick their necks out.

Over the years, the crowd grew from a small band of a dozen or so to a *scene* of forty or fifty people a week. On the big holiday walks, the crowds swelled into hundreds. Many paths crossed in Joe's presence. There were Sufis, Dharma practitioners, Theosophists, Hindu devotees, and Christians. There were also many who had left one of these groups behind, and others who had never belonged to any group and were relieved to find a luminous person who said, with great certainty, that they didn't have to *join* to get the truth.

No one took your name. There was no mailing list. No one collected any membership fee, there was nothing to join. No one pushed any particular code of behavior on you. That was entrusted to karma and your own conscience. No one was held to a set pattern. People came and went according to their own whims or convictions. The walk was simply a marvelous, un-reproducible "happening," an extraordinary testament to the expansiveness of the Millers' awakened hearts.

After dark, the scene shifted to the San Francisco Lodge of the Theosophical Society. Just as the Thursday Morning Walk showcased Joe's unique expression, the Thursday Evening Music Hour showcased Guin's.

In a musty, turn of the century library downtown on Nob Hill, Guin would thank everyone for coming and remind them that **"Whenever two or more are gathered in the Master's Name, He is with us . . . ."** She would play some of her compositions on the piano and Joe would lead the group in singing along. **"Feel, feel, feel for real. No mind makes no deal. Be, be, be still and feel . . . ."**

After the singing, Joe would give a short talk about "*dis-ease*" and getting back into harmony. **"Just by being here together and opening our hearts, we've created an etheric bubble and the JUICE that we've generated can be spread out and used by the forces that are holding the whole world together until we all fall fully awake."**

Following Joe's remarks, Guin would reel off her interpretation of *Lotus Land* composed by one of her mentors, British composer, author and occultist, Cyril Scott. [1] From there, she would launch into her own improvisational meditations with wild riffs that shook the room and sent forth wave after wave of spiritual force, like peals of thunder or tolling cathedral bells.

Next came Joe's solo. Maybe he'd milk a sentimental favorite like

Mother Macree or *Little Bit Of Heaven*, maybe he'd blast off with one of Guin's *Songs To Live By*. These compositions, mostly verses from the world's sacred scriptures, sung by Joe with Guin's piano accompaniment, were the driving force behind their invitation to an "intimate experience of the ultimate." Joe's tenor voice had tremendous power. So did Guin's piano-playing.

After Joe and Guin had established a deep, vibrant atmosphere, they would ask others, their young friend, their "kids," to participate in whatever way their own creativity or inspiration would manifest—singing, dancing, telling a story, reading a poem, playing a musical instrument, or leading a chant. Many who attended the Music Hour gained greatly in self-confidence with flashes and surges of insight. We participated not so much by giving as by receiving, showing the startling change that can be wrought in a single human life when two other beings refuse to see anything but the perfection in that person. [2]

Growing Geometrically

Joe and Guin Miller shared "falling awake" as a common goal. Working together, they said, a man and woman could grow faster, evolving "geo-metrically" rather than "arithmetically." For many, they were a symbol of the spiritual marriage. And it was a real, earthy marriage too, with all its trials and triumphs, foibles, frustrations, and furies.

Guin always said they were "a team." And that's what they were. Everyone heard Joe's joyful harangue. Everyone felt Joe's boundless enthu-siasm. Guin's work was different. [3] She saw it all from a different vantage point. *But they were a team.* Their contrasting styles strengthened them; their contradictory natures presented their young friends with a divine paradox within which a great secret could be discovered.

Guin was Joe's antithesis in many ways. Joe was the son of a house-painter. He grew up in the Midwest, dirt-poor and uneducated. Guin was the daughter of a renowned sea captain. She grew up on the slopes of Mt. Tamalpais, and graduated from U.C. Berkeley.

Joe utilized slapstick, shtick, and corn. Raised with high episcopalian "airs," Guin was far more mannered. Unless, of course, she suspected that you expected a certain behaviour from her, then she would delight in mocking and confounding you. Joe's musical training was barber shop quartets and "girlie shows." Guin's was Chopin nocturnes and Wagner preludes.

Gregarious and extroverted, Joe boasted of suffering from "diarrhea of the mouth." Guin, on the other hand, often spoke nostalgically about the Pythagorean school (which she intimated she remembered). There, she would point out, the students couldn't ask any questions at all for the first seven years of their training, and then even after that, they never asked questions of a personal nature.

Burning All The Furniture

Like any loving parents, Joe and Guin wanted to save their "kids" a lot of trouble. "You don't want your children groveling like slaves, you don't want them below you," Joe said. "You want to lift 'em up on your shoulders and let them reach for the stars!"

Joe and Guin's daring recipe for spiritual freedom was predicated on simplicity, directness, and humanity. No hierarchy, no concepts, no money. No do's, no don'ts, no mumbo-jumbo. Just labor with common sense and a sense of humor. Instead of visualizations, breath control or yoga postures, the Millers stressed the cultivation of a calm attitude, fertilized with your own raw life-experience.

The Millers encouraged everyone to develop their own creativity, to sing or dance with spontaneity and an open heart, letting the "juice" come through just as Rumi's hollow reed sings in ecstasy. Be true to your deepest feelings, and damn the consequences.

Joe's way was Zen without the trappings of Rinzai or Soto, Sufism without hierarchical structure, Christianity without superstition, Theosophy without concepts. To accentuate that message of spiritual freedom, Joe enjoyed bursting into one of Guin's *Songs To Live By*:

> Ignore the opinions of others.
> Let the rumors of your foolishness spread far and wide.
> None of it matters in the least.
> Busy yourself with the burning of all of the furniture
>   in the house of the mind.
> When the job is finished, dynamite the foundations
>   and bulldoze the lot. [4]

"Then, you'll be ready to meditate," he would remark afterward.

Mount Arunachala

Supremely peaceful, wholly benevolent, Sri Bhagavan Ramana Maharshi smiled down from high on the wall above Joe and Guin's fireplace. As the years went on, the large sepia print took on a life of its own. Joe remarked that it never faded. And, indeed, to many visitors it seemed to grow brighter.

Guin often gazed up at Ramana's picture. Communing with his sublime countenance, Guin would smile and let go of her troubles. She would sometimes whisper a few words, then close her eyes to drink the grace. From where? Bhagavan's image felt as if it were a portal into the unseen, all-seeing radiance, through which we could look beyond and, in return, feel the divine effusion flowing from the nowhere into the here.

Joe considered Ramana's teachings to be the exquisite culmination of the quest, the penultimate expression of the divine wisdom for our age. "In a hundred years, what that guy Ramana was putting out will be understood. But it will take that long for people's consciousness to ripen to that point."

The truth struck Ramana at a young age, it overwhelmed him. He ran away from home, traveled to the foot of Mount Arunachala and collapsed there. Years passed before he spoke about his experience. Those who found him dressed him and fed him. Ramana had no guru. He initiated no one. He founded nothing. He insisted any one could realize what he had realized. He did not reject other practices, he simply suggested that since it all ends in the Self, perhaps you can get to that point sooner by dealing with the issue of existence directly.

Simply ask yourself, "Who am I?" Not as a mental exercise, not as a parroted phrase. The inquiry shouldn't be a purely intellectual endeavor. It isn't merely a thought process, it isn't the mental repetition of a question. It is a "diving in," a turning of awareness in upon itself, a sinking, a letting go into the nucleus, that from which the ego arises as the shadow of Sat (pure being).

By forcing the awareness inward when saying "I am cold," "I am tired," "I am sad," and asking "Who is sad?" "Who is tired?" "Who is cold?" And if the answer is, "Well, I am!" then return to the inquiry. "Well, who am I? Am I this body? These senses? This skein of memories? These predispositions?" All these phenomena are transitory, they are subject to alteration or disappearance. But I am not, I just am. Even in deep sleep, I am. But what am I? I return to the waking state and know that I have slept well, although I know nothing else about the elapsed time. When the veil of everything that passes away is removed from my inner sight, what do I see? What am I? The coin is *being alive*. Its two sides are simple awareness and unconditioned love.

In the small pamphlets and other publications that issued from the Ramana Ashram, Joe found corroboration for much of his own experience and predilection. In S.S. Cohen's work, Joe read a statement about something called *Sphurana* that struck very close to home:

> *Sphurana* is felt on several occasions, such as fear, excitement, etc. Although it is always and all over, yet it is felt at a particular center and on particular occasions — it is the Self. If the mind is fixed on the *sphurana* and one senses it continually and automatically, it is realization.
>
> *Sphurana* is described as a "kind of indescribable but palpable sensation in the heart centre . . . ." The apparent discrepancy in its location as "all over" and in the "heart centre" is due to the degree of firmness in, or proximity to the Self. Between the first sensing of the *sphurana* and the discovery of the heart, which is the Self proper, there is only a short lag of time. Therefore, those who are so fortunate as to begin to feel it, should take heart at the imminence of the supreme experience.
>
> *Reflections on Talks with Sri Ramana Maharshi*, pp. 142-143.

Joe felt that these comments from Ramana and his disciple explained a great deal about his own deepening experimentation with the "gentle, in-drawn breath" and the resultant ecstasy. So, in 1971, Joe and Guin wrote S.S. Cohen c/o Ramana Ashram and received an encouraging response:

> *Sphurana* interests only those who are very near the end of their spiritual journey. But to describe correctly the *sphurana*, as you do, is the end itself. [5]

A Sufi is a Sufi if He is a Sufi

The American Sufi master Sam Lewis called himself Marpa and dubbed his friend Joe, Milarepa. The nicknames referred to two ancient yogis who helped bring a Dharma renaissance to Tibet. In the Kargyu lineage, the mantle passed from Marpa to Milarepa. In late 20th-Century America, there was no mantle, only the common ground of two diamond-willed bodhisattvas. Marpa-Sam and Milarepa-Joe were spiritual moonshiners who distilled a potent, contraband brew from the wild American grain. [6]

Sam gave mantras to his students, Joe didn't. Sam had disciples, Joe claimed he himself wasn't even a teacher. Joe had married several times, Sam never did. In the golden age, Joe had Guin for a partner, Sam was strictly a solo act. Sam was a political dissenter. Joe would always burst out into *God Bless America* on the big holiday walks. There were a few other contrasts in style and substance, but both were utterly in love with the reality. Both were untainted by greed or other unsavory appetites. Both just wanted to help people and weren't into wasting anyone's time.

In the remarks he contributed to *In The Garden* (a commemorative volume on the life and teachings of Sam Lewis), Joe articulated the themes of his common endeavor with Sam:

> He [Sam] struck a note that was not Sufism from some other land, but Sufism that became the flavor of the good earth here in the United States itself. It's an important thing . . . .
>
> He was a down to earth person. He wouldn't give you any fancy trip on a nice pink cloud. No, rather than do that, he would kick you and say, now what's the matter with you? Come off your high horse and look at things the way they really are. See things around you as they really are. And realize your at-one-ment with the One. And radiate love to everybody. But no hooks on that love. Nothing taken back. Just let it flow out.
>
> *In The Garden*, pp. 14-16.

Joe often wore the Sufi insignia of the winged heart around his neck. For him, it symbolized the awakening of the heart, the "gentle, indrawn breath and the feeling of love flowing out." He wanted his young friends to strive for a deeper understanding of that awesome power. He wanted them to experience it for themselves. He encouraged them to feel the "juice" rising from their hearts and flowing through their hands. He chose to accentuate feeling over thought. But he wasn't cultivating cloying sentimentality or emotional bias. He emphasized feeling in depth—ecstasy, mercy, joy—the thrill of the divine life resonating from within.

When the Sufi Invocation, "Toward The One . . . ," was recited in his presence, Joe would almost invariably urge everybody to move upstream: **"Not just 'Toward the One,' YOU ARE THE ONE NOW!"** His impatience with the wording didn't mean that he was coming from a deeper place. It stemmed from his indomitable conviction that all seekers could be coming from that deeper place, if they were willing to seize the opportunity.

Joe saw his fellow seekers as temples of the living God, and he exploited the Sufi tradition of the embrace to communicate this attitude. He hugged everyone deeply and purely. Even close to the end of his life, although frail and wobbly, Joe would struggle to his feet to spread his arms and offer his love to each person that entered the room. It was a powerful act and a profound metaphor. He took the seeker in, enfolding the person in a tender embrace. With hearts touching, and heads resting on each other's shoulders, the two personalities were, for that moment, effaced in loving surrender. Hugging the person first on one side, then the other, brought a balance and poise to the act.

Another Sufi custom that Joe borrowed (or "bastardized" as he put it) was the blessing wasifa, "YA FATAH!" The sacred phrase, which contains one of the ninety-nine Names of Allah, means something like "O Opener of the Way". Joe explained it as meaning: "From our hearts to yours!" If it was your birthday or you were embarking on a trip or had just performed or given a lecture, Joe would have the whole group join in "three loud and vulgar YA FATAHS!" In uttering a Ya Fatah, you shout the words and emphasize the Aaaahhhhh! sound. The accompanying gesture starts with your hands folded to your breast, then opening, sweeping outward in a rapid motion. With a sensation like that of a great door swinging wide, you feel a rush of energy pouring through.

For Joe, experiences carried weight, concepts didn't. Joe was looking for passion, kindness, humor, and courage. He didn't put much stock in occult lingo, metaphysics, or psycho-babble. "A SUFI IS A SUFI," Joe often declared in a kind of koan, "IF HE IS A SUFI." He was fond of telling his own version of a story about the Kamal Posh, a rag-tag band of old men in patched robes, who once visited the Prophet Muhammed:

> No one knew where they came from or who or what they really were. They just sat down with Muhammed, and in the Silence, everyone knew. He knew who they were and they could feel what he was really doing and being. After just sitting like that for awhile, the old guys just got up, nodded to him and quietly walked away into the desert. That was his okay to do what he was already doing. And it was all resolved without words or ideas, no "I know this . . . " or "Well do you know this . . . ." No, no. He could

feel from their love where they were and they could feel from what he showed them of his own heart where he was.

Those old men represented a great, watchful presence, the nameless and creedless guardians of human evolution. They weren't affiliated with any organization, they didn't dispense any credentials. They were simply living, burning torches that had been lit from other living, burning torches down through the ages since before the dawn of time.

No Religion Higher Than Truth, No Power Greater Than Love

Both Joe and Guin were card-carrying members of the Theosophical Society. The Society's motto is "There Is No Religion Higher Than Truth," but Joe and Guin "ad-libbed" a second verse, which they declared with relish at the end of Guin's Thursday Night Music Hours, " . . . AND NO POWER GREATER THAN LOVE!"

Without proselytizing or intellectualizing, they *lived* the three fundamental propositions of the Society's essential text, *The Secret Doctrine*, that all is in reality an "unspeakable and unthinkable" Oneness, that life in both its macrocosmic and microcosmic dimensions is cyclic, and that every being must realize the divine for themselves, by themselves and in themselves.

To underscore his no-nonsense approach to the spiritual path, Joe often told an anecdote about one of the Theosophical Society's founders, Helena Petrovna Blavatsky:

> Once in the early days, our beloved H.P.B. was speaking to a group of ladies. They were sipping tea, all gushy and tittering. They wanted the "secrets," they wanted to hear the most "esoteric teachings." "Well, I'll tell you," she said, "the big secret, the key to the mysteries, is common sense, a sense of humor . . . ." Now the little ladies were at the edge of their seats, figuring that the third thing must be quite spectacular. But H.P.B. just smiled and said, "MORE COMMON SENSE!"

What Joe and Guin found in the Society was a comfortable place to hang their hats. The T.S. freed them to work inwardly and serve outwardly without having to adhere to many of the pretenses involved in other "mystical" groups — initiations, codified study, proscribed regimens of practice. For many years, they served on the Board of Directors of the S.F. Lodge, holding the place together until a nucleus of their own young friends were ready to take responsibility for cultivating the atmosphere of **altruism, self-reliance, and eclecticism** which is indicative of Theosophy at its best. The lodge was the Millers' home. They attended meetings three nights a week, year in and year out, until they were too weak to climb up the stairs.

Joe and Guin felt that life was to be lived fully, toiling at the side of one's fellow humans, delighting in their joys, sharing in their sorrows. They didn't want people to "retreat" into temples, ivory towers, or fairy castles. Both sought to cultivate independence and self-confidence in the seekers who came to them for guidance. They felt that beings could and should decide how to work diligently toward their own salvation. "Just look within your own heart," Guin promised over and over again, "You'll find the answers there."

To communicate some notion of what it meant to "fall awake," that realization toward which he exhorted his young friends, Joe occasionally referred to one of his favorite theosophical texts:

> Before the eyes can see, they must be incapable of tears. Before the ears can hear, they must have lost their sensitiveness. Before the voice can speak, it must have lost its power to wound. And before the soul can stand in the Presence of the Masters, its feet must be washed in the blood of the heart.
>
> *Light on the Path*, p. 3.

Demonstrating Mahamudra

Joe's friend, Dr. W. Y. Evans-Wentz, delineated three distinct approaches to the Buddhist teachings; he called these exoteric, esoteric, and *shunyata* (voidness). With the exoteric view, the seeker follows a proscribed course of worship and study that leads to some future realm of salvation or enlightenment. With the esoteric view of Buddhist teachings, the seeker takes initiation with a legitimate guru, receives instructions in meditation, and attempts to transform his being in a course leading through successive stages of enlightenment. With the *shunyata* view of Buddhist teachings, the seeker must relinquish all concepts, renounce all efforts, and die to what *The Diamond Sutra* calls "the idea of ego-entity, a personality, a being, or a separated individuality."

Joe focused wholly on *shunyata* doctrines. The exoteric, with its ritual formalism and intellectual rigors didn't interest Joe, nor did the esoteric, with its arcane lore, guru/disciple relationships and gradations of yogic techniques. Joe's personal understanding and expression of Buddhist philosophy and practice was predicated upon texts such as *The Tibetan Book of The Great Liberation*, which assures the seeker that divine wisdom "instantaneously shines forth" through "unmodified quiescence of mind," and *The Vimalakirti Nirdesa Sutra*, with its admonishment to "view living beings" as "smokeless fire."

Joe, Guin, and their dear friend Sam wanted to cultivate free will, courage, and clarity of mind in seekers. They wanted the young people to brave the unknown, to dare the seemingly Impossible, and to live as adventurers on a great and sacred quest. Joe never discouraged anyone from going into a particular brand of religion or yoga. He would simply say, "If it's working for you, then go with it. If it stops working for you, forget about it." He would add, "Anything I say, or anyone else says, if it makes sense to you, use it, if it doesn't, just leave it alone."

"You don't have do a hundred thousand prostrations or give up meat or sex or contemplate your navel far off in a monastery somewhere," Joe would promise, "Each of you has done all that many times before. What you have to do here and now is be who you really are in depth, not who you THINK you are or who you would LIKE to be but WHO and WHAT you REALLY are!"

Joe was in the business of liberating terms, practices, and practitioners. He didn't say, "Well now, find a teacher you like and go through the preliminary practices and then we'll see." No, he gave out the Six Rules of Tilopa and the River Meditation of Milarepa without asking for preparation or qualifications. "Just go for it, do it! Try it, live it. You can. It's not far from you. It's right there inside you now!"

Joe didn't want people to be patient or to limit themselves or to bow to anyone else. He wanted people to become adventurers, to brave the unknown, to dare. Both Joe and Sam Lewis broke that old pseudo-occult law—"to dare, to know, to be silent." They were Prometheans at heart, they were always stealing the fire.

In one of the fiery letters that Sam wrote Joe from his dive down on the south side of Market Street, Sam enclosed a carbon of a letter he wrote to a colleague, an Anglican minister in England. In it, lovingly, like an older brother, Sam praised and defended Joe Miller:

. . . a miracle took place in this City Sunday night which it may be well to report . . . .

At the end of an excellent cooperative lecture with his wife, she went to the piano and Joseph chanted . . . . He broke loose and demonstrated the Maha Mudra, or the Logos in song, becoming what came out of his mouth.

This is an extreme rarity in the Western world . . . in the audience were several Buddhist initiates, who although Initiates, have not been able to demonstrate the Mahamudra, only lecture on it. Our brother not only lectured but demonstrated . . . .[7]

Futsacutsas of the Kammistram

From the 1960's on, as the youth of the West turned to the teachings of the East, Joe and Guin, as community elders, were at the apex of activity. Intimately involved with the growth of the Sufis, entrenched at the Theosophical Lodge on Mason Street, and only a short stroll from the Buddhist Lecture Hall in Chinatown, Joe and Guin lived in the right place at the right time. Throughout the years, they made deep and wonderful connections with Buddhists, Hindus, and Sufis from the many branches of those great trees.

Joe didn't pay much attention to robes, titles, or grades of initiation. **"You've got to do it for you,"** he bellowed, **"No one else can do it for you."** Of course, he always looked forward to meeting the touring swamis, murshids, and high lamas, and he showed them great respect. He loved to test his mettle against those who were "high on the hog." He called them "the Futsacutsas of the Kammistram" (slapstick slang from his years in vaudeville and burlesque). Joe loved to strike common ground with those from the various mystical traditions. In that way, the circle grew larger, stronger, and more magnetic.

Taking Joe to meet with some "futsacutsa" was a remarkable experience. When he encountered a "REAL ONE," there would be a mystical, non-verbal exchange of energy, an understanding that flowed both ways. "When you come across a guy like that," Joe would comment afterward, "you don't have to say anything, both of you just KNOW." With others, Joe would attempt to "rattle their cages," or seize the opportunity to show the audience something, and maybe send a shock wave through it. He didn't mind making a fool of himself if he could stir a few people on to look a little deeper. But he acted from ecstasy, not disrespect, from free-dom, not jealousy, from love, not conceit. He just wanted everyone to know that there was something wild out in the dark of the auditorium, show the visiting dignitaries that "We're not all just bah bah bah sheep."

At the very least, Joe would burst out with one of Guin's songs or lead the crowd in "three loud and vulgar" *Ya Fatahs*. At the Masonic Auditorium, Krishnamurti asked a purely rhetorical question about love. Joe boomed an irreverently reverent answer down from the rafters. At the Herbst Theatre, he hollered something up from the audience at Ram Dass. Ram Dass closed his eyes, let the eruption of sound cascade through him, and smiled warmly, saying "Hello, Joe." Once, after an "empowerment," Joe challenged the formidable Chogyam Trungpa, shouting "TELL THEM ABOUT THE VAJRA OF THE HEART." Trungpa laughed, "YOU'RE IT!"

One day, Joe went to get Swami Muktananda's "shaktipat." Joe knelt, and Muktananda brushed him with a peacock feather. Joe rose, removed his beret, and sung Guin's composition, "Never The Spirit." Later, after Muktananda suffered a stroke, Joe went to visit him in the hospital. Joe said, "I wanna give you some **SPHURANA**." Muktananda took it in with eyes closed and palms open. He gave Joe a wreath of flowers. When Joe tried to decline the gift and give the flowers back to him, Muktananda said, "No, one must always give offerings to a saint."

From Korea to Konya, from London to Dharmsala, news of the enigmatic Joe and Guin Miller spread with the young people who traveled *in search of the miraculous*. In turn, these adventurers would tell Joe and Guin who was what and when they would visit.

Joe was always looking for the fire in everyone. He wanted to feel the love of the divine and the passion for humanity. Joe wanted to meet beings who had the will to burn and be consumed and set a million more souls on fire. He wanted to reflect the diamond mind and have it reflected back.

Once Swami Satchidananda, Pir Vilayat Khan, Yogi Bhajan, and some of the other "high muckity mucks" were all assembled for a "Holy Man Jamboree." A woman in the audience got into a squabble with Yogi Bhajan. Yogi chided her, telling her she risked "one thousand years bad karma" for tangling with him. Later, during lunch, all the holy men were gathered at a table. When the incident was brought up, Joe shouted at Yogi Bhajan: "IF YOU CAN'T STAND THE HEAT, GET OUT OF THE KITCHEN!" Laughing uproariously, Yogi remarked: "I like the white man." On the way home, Joe asked the young friend who was driving him,

"Do you think he [Bhajan] has it or not?" His young friend, said, "No." Joe shook his head, **"Oh, but he does."**

When Joe met Mata Amritanandamayi (Amaji), he had to sit through long bhajans and make his way through throngs of devotees. Finally, the two beings had an intense encounter. As they embraced, Joe fell into her lap. Afterward, he said, "Wow! Her thighs were shaking. I was trying to give her *sphurana*, but she was pouring it out to me." Joe staggered out with a fistful of *vibhuti* (the miraculous manifestation of sacred substance). Someone said, "Joe, don't spill the ash." Joe answered, "It's all right. I've got hold of what really matters," and placed his other hand on his heart.

Joe supported Sheikh Jelaluddin Loras, son of the great Mevlevi teacher, Suleyman Dede, when he opened up his Sema to women. Jelaluddin bestowed the black robe and hat of a Mevlevi Pir on Joe. During one Sema, Joe led the Sheikhs and Sheikhas in the *Walk of the Prophets*. Joe crossed swords with Sheikh Tosun of the Halveti-Jerrahi over the rights of women. Women were not allowed to practice *zikr* in the Sheikh's circle. It was men only. Joe went down to Redwood City and challenged him, "After all, a woman gave you birth."

In the 1970's, Joe met Nasr Ali Shah. Joe told the following story concerning this meeting:

> I'll tell you about an experience I had. It scared me at the time, but I've realized that I was very lucky to have had it. I went to visit a very special Sheikh that has his own order, I don't even remember his name, but the people of that vicinity, Fairfax, were bringing in to him the fruit of the fields, the grapes and so forth. They were placing it before him with a polite sentence, "This is my offering to you . . . ." They were saying it to him in their own language and I was understanding it! I don't know a damn word of that language. I wondered, "How come?"
>
> Afterward, this Sheikh told the man that invited me there, "Tell him that someday he will be able to do that with all languages." So I thought, "Well, the man has sure given me a goal to shoot at." But what do I shoot at it with, I can't shoot at it with anything. I haven't got enough time in my years to study all the languages. But to be able to just be there, and whatever anybody says, understand it . . . . It gave me proof that I don't do a hell of a lot individually, but the Oneness within me can do it all.

If the atmosphere was stale, staid, phony or overly intellectual, Joe would detonate one of his incendiary devices — but his intent was to revivify, not to destroy. He wanted to lead others by example to the fount of the crazy wisdom.

During a Universal Worship Service at the Palace of Fine Arts, Joe was to represent all those unknown beings who have selflessly tended to the flame of truth through this age of darkness. He asked Pir Vilayat Khan (son and successor of Hazrat Inayat Khan who founded the Sufi Order in the West), to make him a "Madzub." Pir answered: "You are a Madzub, aren't you? I can't make you one. That's what you've always been." And although he was recognized as a Murshid by both S.I.R.S. (the "official" organ of Sam's spiritual legacy) and the Mevlevi Order In America, it was the label Madzub (divine idiot or divine fool) that Joe was most comfortable with and which he used to categorize himself most often. [8]

A year or so before the passing of Joe and Guin, the Dalai Lama visited San Francisco and spoke at the Grace Cathedral. The Dalai Lama is wonderfully articulate. He didn't resort to the use of metaphysical concepts. He never invoked a deity. He didn't refer to any spiritual practice. He said that unconditional love was the universal principle, the common ground. "Look at the new-born child," he said. "It responds to kindness. That's the core. Before the infant learns the least bit about the particular religion or ideology it has been born into, it responds to kindness. This is the core that we must draw on. Compassion is the transforming agent."

I was struck by the simplicity. I realized that Joe had been delivering this message for many years in his own idiosyncratic way. After his talk had concluded, I worked my way slowly through the throng to meet Joe and Guin. As they emerged from the antechamber through which they had passed to take their seats in the vestibule, I saw and felt that something big had occurred. Several of the lamas who had been sitting along side Joe and Guin were looking at them in wonderment. Everyone was sparkling.

On his way out of the cathedral, the Dalai Lama had walked down past the inner vestibule where Joe and Guin had been sitting. All the people rose and stood with their hands in prayerful mudra. The Dalai Lama stepped away from his entourage, walked up to the Millers and took their hands, silently blessing them. For Joe and Guin, that simple, unplanned and unspoken gesture was a kind of final benediction on their lives.

Out and Back. A Draft!

In June of 1990, Joe suffered a serious stroke. Many wouldn't have made it back from that plunge into the abyss. Joe went far out into "the Gnashing of Teeth and the Darkness at the Rim of the World." When Joe emerged, his atmosphere felt like purity purified, his white hair was whiter, his blue eyes were bluer. His body was very fragile, but his consciousness seemed even more powerful and expansive than before the stroke. He told me he knew just what he had already known, but from a deeper, bigger place. Life is a deathless oneness, everyone is inextricably interwoven. Harmlessness is the only power; joy, the inevitable end.

In June of 1992, Joe fell and suffered a head injury. He kept fighting. He didn't want to depart the world. He loved Guin and their work. He felt the hunger of the *sangha* and wanted to keep going, but his physical vehicle had broken down. Will-power wasn't enough anymore. There was suffering and there was rapture.

In the hospital, late at night, a young male nurse came in to draw a blood sample, Joe smiled at him and said, "You don't know it, but I love you. You're part of my pattern too." Early in the morning, the interns visited and Joe burst into a full-voice performance of the "Clown's Lament" from *I Pagliacci*. Later, as he was being wheeled in for a catscan, he blasted the technicians with "MAY ALL BEINGS BE WELL, MAY ALL BEINGS BE HAPPY, PEACE, PEACE, PEACE!"

Back at home, his final few days were an exhibition of courage, surrender and love. His exit was victorious and peaceful. One bright morning, he swept Guin in his arms, as if to take her with him.

In the end, you couldn't slice the moment of departure from the moment before or the moment after. It never happened. The body was simply suddenly no more than an object, a hallowed, hollowed vessel. The being stretched and blossomed into nowhere, the *now here!*

Joe often told the story of Ramana Maharshi's end. The disciples were weeping, they begged him to stay, "Don't go." Gently, Ramana asked, "Where would I go?"

Guin left shortly after her husband. They always said they would leave together. And that's what they did. Joe went on ahead to blaze the trail, Guin took up the rear for the sake of the stragglers. Just as they did on the Thursday Morning Walk.

Guin and I had a few heavy *(no, light)* talks in the pre-dawn hours over her last weeks in the birdcage of flesh and blood. One night I said,

"You're not your body." "No," she agreed. "And you're not your mind." "That's right," she agreed again. "So what are you?" She pondered, then asked in earnestness and delight, "A draft?" It was joyous and liberating view, it was our last uproarious laugh.

Thanks to the Millers' friend, Scott Sadler, who pilots his own small plane, we scattered Joe and Guin's ashes over the Pacific, out beyond Jenner where the Russian River pours into the sea. The trails of white ash billowed, plumed, and spiralled downward, falling from the brilliant blue sky to the brilliant blue waters. A joyous, traceless release. Along with Guin's ashes, we sent the red rose she received as an *apport* in a 1953 seance during which she communed with the soul of her son, a young pilot who crashed and burned in WWII. For many years, Guin had carefully kept the rose in little box inside her piano bench.

Warning

Joe Miller was never at a loss for words. The material from which this collection of talks is condensed is voluminous. Joe also read and enjoyed many books in his ceaseless personal effort to elucidate the spiritual truths. *Great Song's* bibliography provides a snapshot of Joe's own shelf of favorite texts. Many of the footnotes reflect the dog-eared pages and underlined passages that he felt verified his own findings or spoke directly to the needs of Americans in the later quarter of the 20th Century.

Joe Miller qualified everything he said with a disclaimer: **"If you pay any attention to what I'm saying, you're nuts. But if you feel what I'm trying to radiate as I talk, then you're cookin' on the big burner."** Joe also took advantage of every opportunity to remind his friends that **"It can't be found in books."** In other words, the divine reality within the human heart can't be verbally expressed or grasped with the intellect. Whenever Joe spoke the dharma, there was a palpable and indescribable grace in the atmosphere. However, there are books that can help. Joe often said that if there is an attunement between reader and author, something deeper, more profound than words can be transmitted. It can be drawn upon by those with a desire to realize truth experientially.

There is a story regarding the Baal Shem Tov. The Baal Shem saw a demon walking through his house, carrying a book. The Baal Shem asked, "What book is that you have in your hand?" "That is the book of which you are the author," the demon replied. In this way, Baal Shem discovered that one of his students had been secretly writing what the master had said in his talks. When he uncovered the identity of the guilty student and the young man surrendered the notebook, Baal Shem sat down and read it page by page. His final remarks were, "In all this there is not a single word I said. You were not listening for the sake of Heaven, and so the power of evil used you for its sheath and your ears heard what I did not say."

I happily risk the ignoble fate of the Baal Shem's poor student in the hope that these talks will be of some help to those who tread the way of the heart.

Richard Power
February 14, 1993

Ramana Maharshi (above), Joe, serioso,
Guin, here-and-now

Joe singing in the circle

Joe and Guin with Lama Chime Rinpoche

Guin

Guin with her son Leighton, who died in WWII

Joe, rapping in the park

PART ONE:

Falling Awake

Words Stand in the Way of Understanding   *37*
Marriage, Sex, and the Gentle In-Drawn Breath   *38*
Anger   *41*
Practices   *42*
Attachment   *43*
Troubles   *44*
Sahaja Samadhi, Nirva-Kalpa Samadhi, and Drugs   *46*
Sexuality   *47*
Waking, Dreaming, and Deep Sleep   *49*
It's Fun Being Nobody   *51*
Love and Desire   *52*
Evolution   *53*
The River Meditation   *54*
The Six Rules of Tilopa   *56*
Just 10%   *59*
The *Bhakti* Path   *60*
Teachers   *62*
The Spiritual Hierarchy   *65*
Jesus and Muhammed   *66*
The Real I   *68*
Life, the Great Opera   *71*
Spring   *73*

The Mind in the Head Is Just an Outpost   75
We're Not Pushing Any Religion   76
Earthquake!   77
Be Who You Are   79
Thus Spake Ramana   81
The Biggest Problem We Have in the World   84
Theosophy   86
What Do You Want Out of Life?   89
This Too Shall Pass   90
If Anyone Comes to You for Help   91
You Don't Need to Worry
        About the Coming of the New Age   92
Nothing   93
Savoir-Faire   97
Love, the Breath, and Just One Person to Another   102
The Spiritual Teachings of Ramana Maharshi   108
The Sutra of Hui-Neng   117
Sufis Are Seed   125
She Is the Creator   126
Sufism   128
Visiting the Dead (Return of Joe Miller)   132
Broadcast from the Trees (Joe's Last Rap)   135

Words Stand in the Way of Understanding

Words stand in the way of understanding, spiritually speaking. If you use it all to get an intellectual background, that's good. But I once saw a cartoon that showed a man becoming an intellectual. At first, all these words were flying around him. The farther he went, there were even more words and less man. Then finally, just a bunch of words.

You can practice this or that and you can go to a hundred gurus and they'll charge you a moderate sum. Of course, that's unless you want to get the "esoteric teaching," then it might get up to three or four thousand dollars. After awhile, you'll find that nine times out of ten, the advertised "guru" is not a guru at all. He's a business man. But if it comes from the Heart, it's real. People know it! It isn't so much what you say, it's where you are. It radiates out.

You've got to go further into the mirror of consciousness and realize that whatever position you stand in or whatever attitude you may have is but a reflection. We're all living out concepts that we have in our consciousness. If we didn't acquire them in this time, we got them in some other lifetime. But behind it all is the mirror of reality itself. The only way you're going to get there is pure love flowing out. Not by grabbing, not holding or wanting to make it yours, "Oh, this is mine, nobody else can have it."

The mirror is a wonderful symbol because whatever's in front of it, the mirror itself is not affected. You have that within you which reaches and stretches to the reality that's in each of your hearts. When the heart is purified, it sees God, it is God. If there is one place in the physical vehicle you could point to where the reality is living, it's somewhere in your chest, not your head or feet. This is the Immortal I that you can bring alive if you believe in the love of God, not only believing it intellectually but to be it and live it!

Maybe I scare people, maybe I'm a little nuts. I've been called a Madzub. But a Madzub isn't as nuts as people think because he is hearing that eternal and internal music all the time. It's an ecstasy! There is a great song, a great music happening in life at all times. So be the true note you are. Don't let someone else tell you what to do. Be what you are, intuitively, from the depth of your being. Do you want to give me an argument? No? Well, a rolling stone gathers no moss, but it does get a hell of a polish.

Marriage, Sex, and the Gentle In-Drawn Breath

There used to be a gag in vaudeville. We'd say, "What is love?" The answer would be, "Love is a great light." "Well, what's marriage?" "Marriage is the short-circuit that blows out the light." But it doesn't necessarily have to be so.

If you just got married for sex . . . . Well, who didn't? But there's got to be something more than that. A friend of mine once said, if that's all there is to it, you could have gone home and made a bowl of oatmeal and dropped it right in. There isn't any closeness to it. If it isn't a union at all levels of consciousness, feeling and being, it's a most unfortunate thing.

The Tibetans say that when you're married and you're with your wife, you represent the Buddha, the God of the Universe and she represents Tara, all femininity in the world. Then in the joining there is a spiritual lift. It isn't just a matter of getting that momentary satisfaction, but that's great. There is nothing wrong with it. After all, I'm an old man, but even at the age of seventy-eight, there is still fire in the basement. So you've got hope, men. It isn't going to wear out as quickly as you think.

Try to get the feel of it, the spirit in you. In fact, when I hear these ladies that speak of psychology on the radio, I always want to call in and say, "Now look, I know about unendurable pleasure, but how do you make it indefinitely prolonged?" That's what we all want.

In the Chinese teachings of the Tao, they explain that when the explosion occurs, the feelings you have represent the Tao, that's what you will enjoy for Eternity if you'll fall awake! Who wants to fall awake? Yeah, all right. This is what we're heading for. The Indians put it as Sat-Chit-Ananda. Sat is being. Chit is consciousness. Ananda is bliss. Can you imagine living all the time in the way you feel at the height of orgasm? Could you take it? Would you mind trying it?

So if this is what we are coming to, we better take some time getting ready for it. In other words, do a little practice. The dawning of this love flows out not only from one point in the body, but from all points in the body. The hands are considered the parts closest to the heart. We find that most healing is done with strokes or some use of the hands. They're closest magnetically to the heart. But there isn't anything that isn't love if you look at it that way. Can you look at it that way? Can you look at it that way if someone is spitting at you or giving you hell for not doing something you should have done? Can you see that as love? It is. The gimmick is that if it wasn't love they wouldn't want to have anything to do with you. But the fact that they're picking on you or fighting with you shows that there is still attachment. If they become entirely indifferent, you're through.

I found out about that. I lost three wives that way. But I don't think I'll ever lose my present beautiful lady. She might lose me sometime, but I don't think I'll ever lose her. In the other marriages, I figured I would get younger babes. You know, "Why shouldn't I get young meat, I am a man after all." Believe me, it didn't work out. I filled the bill in one way, but I wasn't with them in other ways. For instance, I don't give a damn about going to all the shows in the world or running around or anything like that. I like to just sit at home and eat, watch the boob tube, and have fun. Hell, that isn't a bad life. So if you are contemplating matrimony, try to be friends with the person that you are going to be with. You have to have common interests and still you have to keep interests that are quite different from each other. You don't want to just be a copy, one of the other. Each has got to do their own thing, but you still have to have things in common. The problem is that a man doesn't think of all this at the time.

Of course, ladies, I don't know whether to say this or not, one way to work with a man is to remember that when he's hard, he's soft and when he is soft, he's hard.

You can have ecstasy with just an in-drawn breath with no thought and the feeling of love flowing out. It is not one of these bits where you hold your breath so damn long that you burst a blood vessel or get a hernia. Just a gentle in-drawn breath. But also there is this feeling about it as you draw in that gentle breath, there's love flowing out from the heart. Just breathe gently in. It happens, it happens.

Try it now. Why not? Take a gentle in-drawn breath right now. Go ahead. Let it out. On the outgoing breath, it doesn't happen. By doing this and some other things, you can reach the reality within yourself, at once. It's right there. Maybe not after the first time. It took me years to have it happen a second time. Another way, you see something so damn beautiful that it blows your mind and you're drawn right to it. Just like that, it's right there. I want to pass this on because I believe that in sharing we grow. So I share anything that comes to me that might be of help to other people.

I don't happen to be held down to any sacred vows which say you can't tell these things because this is the esoteric teaching. I'm not into any of that at all. Anything of an esoteric nature is only esoteric because the people don't dig it and can't do it. You don't have to hide anything. It can be right out in the open. If you aren't ready for it, you can't do it and if you can't do it, you can't. There's nobody else holding you back. Ever.

Guin

Anger

When you get mad, go ahead and get angry. Don't think, "Oh, I'm committing a sin." Just get really mad! Then when you get really mad, take the reason out of the way and use the energy that's there. [9]

We each have that point of awareness and aliveness within us. It must be stirred up. When you're singing or you have a belly laugh, it's the same energy. You've activated the aliveness, the energy of the very Oneness. It doesn't have any name on it. It's only in the focus of your own limited mind that you think it's this or that. It isn't.

This power is in feeling, in love. It isn't in thinking. You don't activate the thinking you do. Still, you get a feel about it. So just as a little summation: You can get more stinkin' from thinkin' than you can from drinkin', but to feel is for real!

Practices

I was working down at the burlesque house in the old days. After I finished the midnight show on Saturday, I used to go up on my roof and stay up there until daylight. One morning, I was up there until daylight and just as the sun started to rise, a flock of words came to me and I said to myself, "Now where did I read that?" But I couldn't think of where I had read it and it has stayed with me over a period of years.

> **The manifested universe is the keyboard**
> **upon which the master artist of spiritual reality**
> **plays the symphonic arrangement of life.**

Now that's quite a mouthful, isn't it? If I'd read something like that, surely I would remember it. Now where did it come from? I'm not psychic. It just was Pow! There it is. I've never tried to throw myself into any kind of a fit. I don't do any practices and never have. I don't believe in it.

Oh, once I did. I went up to Chinatown and sat for a couple of weeks with my legs folded up until I damn near killed myself. But nevertheless, I stuck it out. At the time I thought, "Miller, you're a blundering idiot." After all, what good's a pain in the legs going to do your head and heart? That is not what it's all about. If it's a matter of hurting your legs, go get a hammer! Or put your testes on a rock and just tap them. It doesn't make any sense to sit there and suffer. What am I doing this for?

Look, you're using your mind when you're meditating, so what's your spine got to do with it? Oh well, they say, "The Kundalini . . . . " Well, they've built up a great thing about that. But this sort of thing about Kundalini is a lot of hogwash. What you've got to do is come to the Reality itself! Try to reach the Oneness of It and know that the One you're looking for is not out there somewhere but is already inside of you!

Someone asked Rama, "Is it hard to come to enlightenment?" Rama said, "It is and it isn't." He said, "Although we tell them constantly, it's in the heart, few people believe us, but if they would turn to it, they would come to the realization very quickly."

Attachment

You overcome attachment by a change of focus, a change of viewpoint. If you must be attached, be attached to the very essence itself. And if you point at the very essence itself, whatever comes down is no longer an attachment to you. Any argument? No?

These attachments, tell me, who are they pulling at? What is this thing inside of you? Who's the I in it? Your problem isn't attachment, your problem is primarily fear. You're attached to something because you don't want to find that other part. You don't want to have the experience because you're afraid it might isolate you and rob you of the pleasure that you have in the desires that come and go.

You have to just let go of attachments. All of them. Can't you look at it from a contented point of view? From a different level where you're not tied up to that little tassel that you're carrying around? Or bound to some special idea that you learned from some book? Can't you just give it all up and just be? Huh? Have you tried it? What happens when you do try it? It's a pretty nice place, isn't it? It's just letting go. Just let go. I'll tell you what stops attachment quicker than anything else: INDIFFERENCE, indifference to the particular attachment. Indifference is the only power that can get you to let go of attachment. The normal way is that in trying to rid yourself of an attachment, you're against it, you're opposed to it, you find something to dislike about it. You don't want it and you're pushing it away. Well, it's just as present then as when you were attached to it. So the only way through it is indifference.

Can you drop your attachments to things and view them openly, without any bias in a particular direction? Can you look at something clearly? Like a camera takes a picture? Can you make your mind and consciousness like a mirror? To let it reflect back what's up in front of you, so that when it's gone nothing has touched you at all? Because you see, the mirror's still the same. Make your consciousness just that way.

Troubles

I'm not in favor of anybody running away from their responsibilities. You really can't run away. There is something called the Law of Karma, or Cause and Effect. If you walk away from your responsibilities, that's all right. It's just like borrowing money from the bank, you'll just be charged extra interest.

I've got something that is working for me, it's working! I'm healthy! Oh, I'm not prosperous, I'm not important. But I'm contented, I'm full of joy, I'm full of life.

You think you want to be on a power trip, or you say, "Man, I gotta be a millionaire," or "I gotta be the boss." Find contentment first, and everything else will fall into place. First, find that Peace That Passeth Understanding, if you want to put it in Christian terms. It abides in the hearts of those who live in the Eternal. That's now! This is the Eternal.

There isn't anyone alive who doesn't have the feeling that, "Well, that guy's gonna die, but not me. I'm never gonna die." You're sure of it. Unless they say you have cancer and that you're terminally ill. Then you realize something is going to happen. But normally, no one thinks of dying because That part which is the essence never dies.

I believe in the doctrine of reincarnation. I feel we've lived many times before. If we've had so many incarnations, why don't we remember them? Well, if you could remember them before a certain level of tolerance and understanding, the world would be in even more of a mess.

These people from India say, "It's all an illusion." Yeah, it's an illusion, from a certain state, if you get to that state. But don't lean on it until you get to that state. It's a subtle thing, yet it is the most important thing. You've got to find that place of balance within you. Everybody has got it.

So you say, "Yeah, I know that. But you don't know the troubles I've had. It's not my fault." Well, let me tell you something—any troubles you have you richly deserve from somewhere, so you might as well get done with them and be through with it here and now.

Most of you seated here haven't reached the half-way mark in the number of years I've gone through. I'm trying to help you get a jump on these experiences. I want to help you look at them. But you can't change anyone. I can't change you. Everyone has to do it for themselves. You have to find it for you and your only responsibility is for yourself.

Once you get yourself running smoothly, as far as you're concerned, the whole world will be running smoothly. And the biological urges? Nothing wrong with them. They're healthy.

Sahaja Samadhi, Nirva-Kalpa Samadhi, and Drugs

Nirva-kalpa samadhi is being unconscious and in an ecstasy, but with no awareness. But *sahaja* is when it's in the natural state and you remain within the center of your consciousness with awareness of everything that is happening on the outside.

In *sahaja*, you're aware of everything, yet it doesn't change the fact that you're at one with the reality itself all the time. You still have thoughts like anybody else, thoughts that bug you, but they're in a quiescent state and stay at the periphery of the thing.

Nirva-kalpa samadhi is another way to go to sleep and enjoy the ecstasy. You've got to have it with the consciousness, otherwise you don't have anything. If it were just a matter of going to sleep to be enlightened, everyone could go to sleep and that would be it. Ramana Maharshi states all this very clearly.

The drug experience is a distortion in which you are using something out of the unconscious. Whether you're projecting it in the particular way you formally experienced it or it's distorted, it's still an imaginary thing. It is a projection of the imagination. True *samadhi*, *sahaja samadhi*, is an awareness in ecstasy at all times. It's a total awareness with no biases connected to it.

One more thought concerning acid trips, at least those who have gone through that experience are aware that there is another phase of consciousness beyond the one they are ordinarily in. The young people who have come to me were those who had these experiences and then decided, "Well, if there is this other dimension I can get into, surely there's a way to get into it without drugs, in a perfectly natural way." So those who can take it in the natural way are satisfied and don't take the acid or smoke hay anymore.

Sexuality

Now I don't know whether Muhammed was celibate or not, but he was married to twelve different women after his first wife died. Now I suppose he could have said, "All of you sit down and pray." But if Muhammed was half the man I think he was, he was using the facilities at hand!

And in all the books of the Old Testament, you find they had a few concubines on the off-beat. To give you a specific view on that, King David was very aged, they thought he was going to pass away, so they sent to a nearby village and got a young virgin of sixteen summers and laid her on his bosom and he lived for five more years after that.

There's a purpose that can be holy and uplifting, if it's not selfish. You're sharing! Sex can be used as a means, just as eating or meditating can be used, a means to refine you more and bring you into that space. What I feel from inside is that those of you who are here in this room and people in this country at this time are the seed of a new world. And that you can help tremendously in this way, by making it a holy thing. If you don't desire that sort of thing, okay. But to abstain from something because you think it's going to make you more holy is selfish. **The rule is—universal love!**

I remember reading something in a book on this particular subject. I didn't try it. It said that if a man found himself in an excited condition, he should take two little bowls, one filled with hot water, the other with cold water and dip his testes into them. It would damn near kill you, I figure.

But can you see the yin and yang? It can be a temple of union between man and woman lifting them to the highest! Remember that lady of Rama's, she was looking around for him and instead of saying, "Where's Ram? Where's Ram?" she was using her own name?

If you want to go the other way, there have been many saints that went the celibate way. But I'm not so much in favor of saints. I prefer sages. Because they had saints in every great religion, but some of these were, to my way of thinking, very fanatical. A sage is someone who has to be a saint as well as have the other understanding. So we take it where it is.

For instance, I hug everybody when they come in. And I'm sure that I am more intimate with those people in embracing them, heart to heart, and by giving them a silent "Ya Fatah!" with my whole being than anybody that's ever been in bed with them.

Love can lift you up! It can lift you up or tear you down. It can be lower than the dogs that run in the streets or higher than the angels. It's up to you. If you don't want to use it, okay. But I don't think it'll ever go out of style. [10]

Waking, Dreaming, and Deep Sleep

It's there all the time. You're never away from it. Okay, let's take the business where you go to sleep at night. You put in a day's work, maybe it's been a rough day and so forth. Okay, you've had your dinner and you've sat down, maybe you've had sex, maybe not. Anyway, you decide it's about time to go to sleep. When you finally get to that little edge of falling asleep, the thoughts of the day aren't there. Everything is quiet. And you feel just like you did when you were a little kid and you'd wake up in the morning and say, "God, what a beautiful day it is." We go through this cycle every day. We live, we're born, we die, we reincarnate for the next day. You're having a little death each day.

So you go to sleep, you dream. Your dreams are usually a distorted expression of things you haven't settled during the day. Then you go into deep sleep. Of course, people come over and tell me they have prophetic dreams. Some of them are, some of them are not. They're just a distortion of what they have been living in the daytime. They didn't get an answer, so they're working it out on the subjective plane. They have their own movies, they're running their own tapes. When they come to me and ask about them, I can usually explain and they see how it fits in.

Sometimes you just get mixed up in that looking glass. If there's a twist in that looking glass, you get awful surprises. I stopped in a cheap hotel one night and woke up to look in the mirror, I thought, "No, that can't be me."

When you have your dreams, you have washed out a little of what has happened during the day. Next, you go into what's called deep sleep. You don't remember that. You say, "Well, I'm not there." But if you wake up the next morning and somebody asks you can you tell them whether you slept well or not, how the hell do you know it? There must be a part in the depth of your consciousness that never sleeps and is always aware. If you get to a point where you can keep your consciousness focused, you can go through the whole period of falling asleep, dreaming, deep sleep and back awake again without losing that awareness. Now when you can do that, you're cooking on the big burner.

The first time I tried to do that was in the city of Chicago and I had been studying these books about keeping your consciousness centered, so you'll know where you are all the time. Okay, so I kept my consciousness centered. Well I felt myself going to sleep and I found out that my wife was right when she said I snored. I do. But I still was holding that consciousness. And it seemed as if there were different roads like a pie out to all kinds of different places. I could go some way, but no, I held it there. Okay, now I'm going to see if you really get out of your body in deep sleep. Then the phone rings. I thought, "Gee, I gotta answer the phone." So I jump out of bed and fall flat on my butt. So much for inquiring into other dimensions.

But you can develop the awareness and sometimes you can do it in the dream state. Sometimes you can change your dream. But if you try to do it too violently, it'll wake you up, but if you just insinuate yourself into it, you can change your dreams. Now there is a whole dream yoga among the Tibetans. If you can do it, that's great. I've done it a couple of times. But on the other tries, I missed completely. Anyway, these are just things to experiment with. Your awareness is all!

It's Fun Being Nobody

You all had to be a little bit off the beam or you wouldn't have even come here in the first place. But I am going to try to get to you what it is that makes me feel the way I do. First of all, I'm nobody. It's fun being nobody. Then you know that everybody is you and you're everyone else.

When you talk to someone you don't feel any gap between the two of you. Instead of just a conversation, you feel communion. You're talking from your heart. You quit playing games off the top of your head. Unless you want to be a con man. But in that case, even when money comes your way, you'll usually throw it away as fast as you get it. We don't want a con, we want the real thing.

Each one of you have multitudinous answers to every question. All the books you see on the walls around us don't carry one-hundreth part of THAT which is in the depth of your own being. But don't think you're going to get it by just controlling your sex force and becoming bramacharya. I'm sure that nine out of every ten people here have gone through that experience in other lives. Now you can bring the essence of what you have found there and realize it here in the midst of this circumstance. [11]

When you come to a place in your life where there's a bind or something in your way, just take a gentle in-drawn breath and give it a blessing. You don't have to get down on your knees and hold your hands up or make the sign of the cross or even pull your belly in. It's how you are inside and how you're living in this world that matters. The eternalness is within, everyone has that spark!

We're all going through a school and it's so deadly serious and dramatic. So few of us can just lean back and look at it. Observe what happens. See what you want. The main thing that everybody wants is happiness. If I find someone who doesn't want happiness, I call the nearest headshrinker.

Love and Desire

Now what is love? We are creatures of love. None of this world would be in existence without it. It's that subtle something that we feel inside. It's those moments when you say, "That's a beautiful scene, a gorgeous sunset." And in those moments what happens to you? You can't make it a thought, you can't put it into words, but something lifted you out of yourself. This is what love in its purity is. It is radiating out. [12]

When you want to possess somebody, it's perfectly natural. But that's desire. And desire is pure energy. You need that energy. Admit that. But love, pure love is a matter of feeling. You are that love now. We jump around and go to dozens of people but everything we're looking for, we already are at this point in ourselves. It's a matter of getting things out of the way, so that IT can function through you.

Evolution

The evolution is only for the outer vehicles we're wearing. **Each of us, with that spark of Infinity within us, is pure fire from the one heart of love.** That's already pure. It doesn't have to be made pure. It's already reality.

All we're doing here is finding out about these instruments. **At some future time and place, we'll have grown to a stature where our bodies can be an entire planet and all the humanity the same as the particles within our physical bodies now.** We'll know about all that when the life itself is love. Love and life are one. That part is already pure in each of us. But we're going through this to find out about the evolutionary facet, the desire to become aware of ourselves. We are becoming aware of our Infinity and our oneness with the Reality.

The path which the spiritual aspirant can follow is like the gate that they depict in oriental things. It's no gate. It's no path. You individually are the path and we're the temples of the living God. Turn to that God and you'll get a hotline to the reality which is God and you'll know.

The River Meditation

Now this is the River Meditation of Milarepa:

> **When the mind is left in the primordial,**
> **unmodified condition, knowledge dawneth;**
> **When this condition is maintained, comparable**
> **in its calmness to the flow of a calm river, knowledge**
> **in its completeness is attained. Wholly abandon**
> **all directing and shaping of thoughts. Ever**
> **maintain quiescence of mind, O Yogin.**
>
> *Tibetan Yoga and Secret Doctrine*, p. 150.

Now let me explain a little further about all of this. Nobody gave me a look as if to say, "What the hell are you talking about?" So I guess you have all done this to a certain extent. Just watching the thoughts go through the mind. But probably because of your own emotional fixations, you pick up on the ones that you're all excited about or that you hate some aspect of. Now the fact that all of you admit it is possible to watch your own mind, makes me just ask one thing—Who's doing the watching? Who is it? Most people say, "My mind, that's me," and all silently acquiesce and agree that you can do this. If you don't do it and use it, it's up to you. Regardless of what comes down, no matter how much it bothers you, you can still get to that place and just look at it.

And another thing, when you meditate, you don't have to tie yourself in a knot. As long as you're working with your mind, it doesn't make a damn bit of difference if you're sitting in an upright position or not. One of the most advanced human beings at this late period, I.K. Taimni said, "Look, when you're in meditation, you're using your mind, so make your body comfortable." You can do it lying flat on your back. Of course, this disagrees violently with the teachings we get from some of the Buddhist groups, particularly some of the Pure Land groups. The idea of meditation isn't to develop your muscles or tie them in a knot. It's so damn silly when you think about it! That's not what it's for. Meditation is for you to calm your thinking. You can do it. You know the only thing that keeps you from doing it? Your feelings. Feelings associated with your personality, not the feelings spoken of in the *bhakti* teachings.

The only thing we need, that everybody needs, is to be able to handle our feelings as well as we can handle our minds. It's your feelings that hurt you. It's not your mind in particular, you can always shift to something else. "Become desireless, become non-attached," this is something you get strongly from the eastern world. It's because in the early days, they realized that feelings are the things that throw you, your feelings are the things that mess you up and make you neurotic. Their recommendation, from the *bhakti* standpoint, was to drop all desires except the main one—love of God. Then let it all pour out that way.

Another thing that most people think is that when you practice meditation, it has to follow a certain pattern. Well, it can follow a certain pattern if you want it to. You can take a piece of clear glass and place it on any color and it will be the color of whatever you place it on. You can clear your mind. Just let it be still. You can place your mind on any subject and look at it in all its facets, if you don't allow your feelings to interfere. You can see all sides and phases of it. Now if you can all sit and do the River Meditation, then you can be there.

You can use this particular meditation given by Milarepa. You figure within your consciousness, within your mind, that you're sitting beside a river and that what's coming down the river is all kinds of thoughts, multitudinous thoughts, and you don't try to turn them off. You don't try to make yourself a blank, you just look at the thoughts, but you don't grab at them or try to push any of them away. Just observe it all. After you've just observed for a while, no matter how many waves there are on the river, it'll all calm down. Just watch it. It's called the River Meditation of Milarepa.

The Six Rules of Tilopa

Concerning this nirvanic path, the most important thing to remember is the Six Rules of Tilopa:

> **Imagine not, think not, analyze not,**
> **Meditate not, reflect not, keep in the Natural State.**
>
> *Tibetan Yoga and Secret Doctrine*, p. 130.

Anyone care to volunteer in telling me what that means?

I think it's meant as a kind of synthesis of understanding. If you can dig it, you'll have something that will last you the rest of your life—the idea of being able to keep your mind in the natural state. This doesn't mean forgetting what you have learned, it doesn't mean throwing away the knowledge. But bring it to the *natural state*.

When Tilopa speaks of the *natural state*, it's the same as when the Zen people speak of No-Mind. In other words, you're not saying something in your subjective mind all the time, you're not working on it constantly. Whatever you're doing, you're letting the mind be at ease. Let it be in a place where it's aware, but it is not biased in any direction, so you can use it as a tool. See? "Imagine not, think not, analyze not, meditate not, reflect not, keep in the natural state."

All the things you'd usually do with your mind, it's saying, "Don't do any of 'em." It seems a contradiction, but it isn't. It's giving you a pattern, a way in which you can hold your consciousness, so that whatever comes up or wherever you are, you're at ease and you're free. This way you don't have anything of a subjective nature bugging you. The Six Rules are trying to bring to your attention that nirvana, heaven, and all the glorious places in this world come from one source and are, in reality, a Oneness.

I don't mean to discourage anybody from going to another part of the world in order to find something, but if your consciousness would reach a place of realizing this Oneness, you wouldn't have to go anywhere to **BE** there! You're there now in this point that you are here. When you take yourself to another place, the environment will have an effect on you. But really whatever you are thinking in your consciousness and whatever thoughts you've been going over, you're taking them along with you! It doesn't matter, it doesn't make any difference where you go. All you're getting is an outward change of things.

Look, what you want to find is more space inside yourself. You want to feel that part of you inside that is free. It is free! Except for what you put on it. Suppose you are thinking, you're worried. Suppose you have a difficult situation to work out. Maybe some work to do. Well, after you've done your best at trying to figure it out, if you keep hanging on to it, you're just using up extra gas. You're not doing any good; you're not getting anywhere with it. Look it over. Make the decision. Then drop it.

Most of the things that we worry about never come to pass anyway. Unless we do something to encourage the worrying and add a little jab on the off-beat and then sometimes it comes true. Then you're as lousy as you think you are or whatever it might be. You've got to understand that it's all a Oneness.

All the material things, all the so-called spiritual things, it's all an actual Oneness. You say, "Well, Heaven's over there," or "Nirvana is over there." Look, on any of the trips the boys took to the moon, did they find anything out there? You've got to have that place inside of you. It's alive! Of course, some people aren't as alive as others, but it is still there.

The thing is not to look for something outside yourself, or think that possessing some particular thing is going to be of help to you. Whether it's a car or a home or whatever it is. You may satisfy some of your desires in your lower mind, but if you don't have contentment, you'll be very unhappy. We have few millionaires who are particularly happy. Though I think I could have a million dollars and be quite content myself. I think you feel the same way? But would you? Or would you be grasping for more? If you had some of the things that other people have, do you think you'd be happy?

You have to find peace and contentment within yourself. That is the most important thing. If you want to put a religious name on it, that's up to you. But you have to find peace and contentment within yourself, that's the most important thing! We have all kinds of names to put on it. But the basis of it is love, you got to feel love pouring out — **unselfish love**. If that isn't there, the rest of it usually doesn't come down. Do you really understand that there is a part of you which is Immortal, which is never born and never dies? You are just part of the Oneness of it all. That's the important thing.

Now I'm not tearing down intellect, because I think it's fabulous. You can use it in so many ways to help bring yourself around so that you understand who you are. In other words,

As a thing is viewed, so it appears.

The Great Liberation, p. 232.

Any personal situation, business situation, religious or social situation, okay, look at it. Instead of being on the periphery of the circle, if you have a proposition or want to look over life, figure you're standing in the middle and looking at all of it. You can see all the relative points of view concerning any given situation. Your viewpoint has to be right, if your viewpoint isn't right, they'll just drag you around by your nose and do anything they want with you. When somebody tells you something, if you don't think that's it, don't mess with it. To hell with it!

And what do you want? What did you come here for? You say, "Oh well, I want to know about this or that . . . . " Okay, okay. Nevertheless, you didn't buy a book, so you didn't want that as much as what I've got that you can use! And I don't mean my pink and white body, it's too old for that generally speaking. It wouldn't stand up over a period of time; it'd be a lot of fun for a short while. What did you come here to get? Is it the happiness that I feel? The vibes that I put out? Is that it? Well, that's what each of you have inside yourselves and only you stand in the way of letting it come out. There's nothing that I have that you don't already have. It just depends on what you want to do with it.

Just 10%

I tell people to keep a little place, just 10% inside in your heart and know that little place doesn't belong to anybody, just God and you have access to it. Keep that as an overtone all day as you're doing your stuff. You're at one with that reality within you. It doesn't disturb anything else you're doing; it just gives you a subsidiary overview of the whole thing, whatever is coming down. Then you'll get to a place where you're imperturbable, no matter what occurs. You can find that place within you where you can look at things and live them that way.

So that old remark that all of you probably made when you cut out from the square world to begin with, about "hanging loose," was well and good. But what you did was take on another establishment, the establishment of that which you went into, and then, clung on to that just as much as you ran like hell from the established things previously.

You don't have to look anywhere outside yourself because you carry the exact and perfect truth within you. The Master Jesus said, "Be still and know I Am God." In other words, you're faced with a situation, so take it from the slap and go the way your heart tells you to go. If you are not tied up with hates and dislikes, you'll be living right from that point. That's it!

This isn't something that you can go to India and get, or the moon, or South America to get! Huh? It's inside you. Just be still and find it and start living from there.

The Bhakti Path

The essence of the *bhakti* way, the way you're all going, is to realize that LOVE that is so intense and far stronger than any sexual experience you'll ever have. It's just flowing out of you to everyone. That's what you got coming up for yourselves. And I mean you feel it flowing out to everyone, regardless of who they are, not because of who they are but in spite of who they are. You feel the Oneness. It's not a matter of communication in words, it's a communion of spirits. And man, if you start living it that way, you don't have to worry about moving the Kundalini up to flip your lid. To hell with that! You've got something greater than that—you've got something that will last.

You're trying to do something with your mind that the mind wasn't equipped for.

If you're going the *bhakti* way, you don't have to bother with any of the teachings of yogas or anything else. Just devote yourself supremely to love! To love in its essence. Realizing that love is where it all comes from and the source itself, pure devotion. But it's not pure devotion toward any individual. It's not only devotion, it's trying to live it as well! That kind of thing can't be touched in words because you've gone to another level. You can't explain the abstract in concrete terms.

The feeling that is truly coming from the heart is from the higher mind. And that is why I always tell you not to pay a damn bit of attention to what I'm saying, but try to feel what I'm radiating out to you. When you go the way of *bhakti*, it's by the grace of God. It just starts happening. There it is, you've got it. [13]

You don't have to know why or where or who. It happens. It's because it's coming from the heart. The heart, at least from what I've read—and I'll stand on *The Siva Sutras* [14]—is that point within you of universal consciousness, that light point within you where you can touch the universal being. It's in the heart. And your mind, although it is of that same consciousness of the Oneness, is confined with the thoughts and the living you have done in your many incarnations—also what your folks have put on you, what society has put on you. But the other part of consciousness is universal.

All of us reach to that universal part now and then. When we do reach it, there is always a big lift that happens and we think, "Well, I'm not good enough for that." Who isn't good enough for anything? The only thing that's holding you back from understanding the inner part of your own nature is yourself and the blocks you put in the way. Any troubles you've got, remember it's either something you have earned or piled up on yourself karmically or it's your attitude and viewpoint about it which is keeping you from getting clear of it.

Teachers

Most of my teachers have been life. Life itself is the teacher. In other words, it is the God within that I am living by. I surrender to that. I surrender to the love of the One which teaches me from within.

I went to see a Murshid (teacher) who came here from Iran. And so he asked me some questions on this teacher stuff. He said, "Do you believe in common sense?" I said, "Yes, as long as it does not violate what I am getting from within, from my heart." He said, "Did you ever have a master?" I said, "Yes, it's within and everywhere else. Where isn't it?" He said, "How do you run your life? Is it by what you think, is it logic and common sense?" I said, "As long as it doesn't violate that which is within." He said, "Have you ever surrendered to anyone?" I said, "Yes, to the God within." He was talking through an interpreter and he said, "You know, most people prefer common sense, but you're crazy." And so, through the interpreter, I said, "Thank you." Then he said, "But I'm crazier than you are."

So much for teachers, although my reading has been very broad. When I was a kid I would try anything that came along, including even the famed black magician, Aleister Crowley.

I don't consider myself a teacher. I consider myself a friend and that's the way I have always dealt with people. I look at it this way, one on one, that's where something happens. Sometimes it happens with a group, but that's not because you have communication. It is because you have communion. [15]

The most important thing is what you don't say. It works because you're acting as a wide open place for that to flow out to others of like spirit. And in what you're saying, it may be the way you're saying it, the tone of the voice, the music that's in it. As Inayat Khan was always mentioning, everything is music!

So I don't have any credentials. Although I'm a Minister, I'm a Buddhist Priest, a Dharma Master, I'm a Swami, and I think I'm a Madzub in the Chisti Order. It's the universal aspect that counts.

However, if anyone comes up to me and says, "I'm studying such and such a place," I say, "Is it helping you try to understand life more fully? Are you growing from it?" Never try to pull anyone away from the particular thing they are doing. I encourage them. On the walk, we have kids from every known and unknown outfit showing up and that's perfectly OK.

It isn't in being a stooge that you come to it. It's the heart to heart thing. That's where the real transmission comes. But the meaning of transmission isn't that the teacher gives you anything. All he does is act as the reflector, so that the light that he has, or the mirror which he is, bounces back into you and you'll put out a little more.

So you read all the books. But when you read a book, even if it's an author someone else might not think worthwhile, if you're feeling an empathy to that author, you're feeling what he was trying to say but couldn't write. That's when you start getting it from him. You're tuned in to that. You have a communion with the inner part of the one who has written the book. See what I mean?

The truth IS, nobody can say it. You've got to BE it! You've got to live it. That's Sufism, that's Theosophy, that's Christianity, that's Vedanta, Zen, Buddhism. Whatever name you want to put on it, you have to feel the at-one-ment with the reality. Your surrender is signing off from personality and ego standpoint, then living from the One. The inspiration is always there. Mind is a wonderful tool and must be developed. But it's a lousy boss. You've got to go up to headquarters and let it come from there. Then, whatever happens, you can speak with spontaneity.

If you're going along the street and you start talking with someone, your mind tells you one thing, but your heart tells you something else. If you can feel it, you know where you are and where that person is. Little kids can tell who likes them and who doesn't. So can dogs. It's a natural thing that we've covered up. We should be able to know it. But those of us who are anywhere near IT have also taken on the responsibility, in this time when things are coming down, to try radiating enough so that it will impinge on the ones who are ready and start opening the center of their beings. It doesn't make any difference what you're talking about. If you really come to a harmony with what you feel inside, you know something is happening.

When people come to the Music Hour or go on the hike, if something is really happening for them, then they can walk down the street and if they go by someone who's feeling lousy or depressed—they don't even have to say anything—it's quite possible the person will say, "Why do I feel better? What happened? Maybe the physic I took is working." You have to BE.

It's all in that little word, **BE**. A Sufi, a Buddhist, a Theosophist has to **BE**. And then you contact the light that is in you. BE . . . BE . . . BE! So much for teachers.

Sure, I've read a lot. But I have never surrendered myself completely to anybody. I'm not that particular kind of person. It isn't that I don't feel great veneration for many teachers and the many who I've met that are not called teachers, but are nevertheless giving out the light.

If you set the compass of your being right, there isn't anything or anyone you encounter that you don't learn from. My friend Sam said, "If I'm a Murshid and I'm a great teacher, it isn't so much what I gave the kids, it's what the kids gave me." If you're going to start yelling something to someone, you should dig what's coming down all the time, even in the intimate association of just talking with someone. It's all multitudinous tints of the Clear Light, if you want to put it in those terms.

See, whatever school a person is going through, give respect to that school. Never tear down any teaching. Because, if they are getting something out of it, well and good, or if it dries up on them and they're not getting any more juice from it, they'll split anyway. Leave them alone. But help them as much as you can from within their own frame of reference.

The beautiful part of it is that there is no limit to what you can give, if their hearts are open to the love of God. And love of God means love of everything. It means that you just open it up and leave it open. Nothing can hurt it anyway.

The Spiritual Hierarchy

(Question: Could you speak about the spiritual hierarchy and the spiritual government of the planet?)

I could, but I won't. I'll tell you why. This is the way I look at it, "Everything is vibration." That's a quote from Inayat Khan and science as well. We have the possibility of coming to full enlightenment and falling completely awake on the planet. There are hierarchies and a person who believes in the hierarchy, most of the time is using it as a leaning post. That's the reason Zen eliminated it. No hierarchy.

There is a spiritual hierarchy and there are spiritual beings, of course, living on all the other dimensions. But it's not worthwhile to make much of it here. Some people and in some teachings I know of (I get all the advertising from every hokey outfit that's going) are trying to bend you into leaning on an idea. [16]

The real spiritual hierarchy is there, but we grow to that. If one of those guys pays attention to us, we'll know it. But it's funny, we go into their world. They don't come into ours because you're not ready for it if you're not in a place where you can lift your heart to that point and touch that. If you can, you know it. You don't have to have somebody tell you or say this is Futsacutsa from the Kammistram!

Jesus and Muhammed

(Question: I have heard people say that you can't come to complete enlightenment while incarnated in this body. Is that true?)

That belief is primarily an Indian thing and it's not true, it's definitely not true. If it were true no one would have ever written the Vedas, we would never have had Moses, we would never have had Abraham, we would never have had Muhammed.

After all, let's just look at J.C., Jesus, okay? Here he is in a lousy little country and Rome is ruling all the known world at the time. And he's got the hippies of the day following him. Okay? And you can figure how elevated he was when he rode into Jerusalem on his ass. Right? And he even had somebody steal that and bring it to him and not say anything to the people who owned it. Huh? But still, **he had IT!**

Look at Muhammed. Here is a guy who doesn't have any education. He doesn't even read or write. He meets a middle-aged woman who's got enough loot, so he can live comfortably. He marries her. I mean these are very human people.

So he goes ahead out to this cave and he doesn't even know if he's in meditation or not. He is just sitting there and all of a sudden, this figure shows up in front of him and hands him a book and says, "Read it!" He can't read. But the figure says, "Read it!" So he read, then went home. Now his wife is carrying him along as a spare, okay? He goes home and says, "I talked to an angel." Then he says, "Don't tell anybody." How many women do you know that you could say that to then have it broadcast all over the place. So I figure by the very fact that he said, "Don't tell anybody," was his first great psychological move. So it went out, of course.

He learned a lot from that angel in one afternoon. But you can't make him up as any kind of saint. And you can't make Jesus into any kind of plastic saint. He went into the temple and blew his cork and lost his temper and ran everybody out of the joint. What if somebody went down to Montgomery Street and went into one of those buildings and started chasing the people out? So Jesus had his human side, but he also had the love of God in him and it wouldn't stop. Muhammed had the same thing in him. It wouldn't stop. He had something that was coming out of the

Oneness.

It wasn't somebody very elevated who spent his whole life contemplating his navel or living in some monastery. In fact, none of our great teachers came from such a background. No. They came up out of the mud, the same as the lotus grows and the dewdrop falling on the lotus is like a pure diamond. So who knows, if you open your hearts, what kind of rubies and jewels of spiritual attainment can come from every one of you. All right, you don't know. Try it. You might like it. Live by being. The greatest things in the world have come from people who had no background and weren't set up as important enough to do any such thing. But when you're touched with the reality, you DO IT! You LIVE IT! And in the meanwhile, you live it TO the reality.

The Real I

The body isn't the sentient part of you. When you're asleep, you don't see, hear, or smell. It's this spirit, or soul if you wish, THAT which animates all of our being so that we are aware of all these things. When a person is what we call "dead," the spirit has left; there is no reaction from any part of the person. So the real you, the real I, is using the body. It also is the body here and now, but It is the essence Itself, the I within. I say it's the I-I because most of us are drunk. We think the I is Richard or Rashida. Richard thinks it's Richard, Rashida thinks it's Rashida. Huh? Each one of you according to the name you are called thinks that I is you. But it isn't you!

The Real I is in this Mahamudra we're talking about, it's in the greater depth. That I is always there. It is never born and never dies. That I is Eternal. When you wake up in the morning, you don't say Rashida is awake or Richard is awake. No! You say "I'm awake." Huh? Can you imagine using your given name? Nah! It's I, I . . . .

So that I is something that is right here and now. So is the Eternal Reality here and now, if you can but realize it. If we weren't drunk and thinking we're only our physical vehicles and the incarnations behind us that are holding to it, we would realize that this I is a Oneness including everyone and that we are each one an individual part of the I-ness. In other words, this I is a limited expression of universal consciousness. This ordinary I that you use all the time . . . .

We make it so complicated. My God, look at all these books and in each one of the books somebody figured they knew exactly how it was. But it was only their view of it. If you should come in here someday browsing and find a book with which you feel an empathy, a closeness to the person expressing through it, then you might be able to reach back through the book to get to what the guy really meant when he wrote it. It's never in the actual words themselves anyway. It's between them and around them.

I read something in Inayat Khan which tickled me; he said, "Mysticism cannot be taught. It must be realized." Well, what I have been saying for years is that It can't be taught, it has to be caught! That's the way with it.

But we make it so complicated. It gets even more complicated with people who go to most groups. For instance, I read something that said, "Well, maybe in three or four incarnations, you might reach it." You're either there now or you're never going to be there! It is that very part of you that is the life and essence itself. But there is much ado about it to try and bring you to the place of Mahamudra where you can see it clearly, in the natural state. Then you realize that whether you're wearing the body you have now or some other body, it wouldn't make any difference because the I-I of you, the I that is not drunk, will always be there.

They say, "You gotta get rid of your personality, you gotta get rid of your ego." You don't get rid of your personality! Your personality is something that you have built-up with all you've learned in different incarnations and all your capacities. No two people's capacities are the same. You don't lose that. But you begin to realize that you are not a separate part. You're One with All of It! Yet still individual in expression.

You should live it from the Heart. The God within you is the essence. All you have learned in any incarnation, you can use right now through the I-I within you. It's funny, when you put your hand on your chest and feel the heart going ba-BUMP, ba-BUMP, it's saying "i AM, i AM." Pay attention to it! Pay attention! The clock's running. It's later than you think. Okay?

Another thing, you have to be able to retain this awareness twenty-four hours a day and the time will come when you will be able to retain it. I mean you're thinking but you're aware of what is happening consciously. And if you get so that you are aware to that extent, then if you want to travel anywhere, you can go anywhere you want in one of your finer vehicles. But you don't get to that awareness if you're thinking of using it to be in any way harmful or vengeful or anything like that. You don't come to that awareness unless you become ripe enough.

And so when the time comes for you to pass away, you feel it intuitively. You know it's time and you just step out and leave the body. Like this guy in India, Tagore. He had a few of his friends in the night before and had a big party. He said, "I'm leaving tomorrow." They came down in the morning and he went in and laid on the couch. When they came in ten minutes later, he had left.

There was nothing for them to feel sad about. He knew where he was going. He knew what he was going to be doing. And they knew he knew. He told them himself.

If the time comes for me to throw away a shirt or a pair of pants, I say, "Well, I've gotten all the wear out of them I'm going to get. I better toss 'em." Gee, I don't cry crocodile tears because I'm throwing away a pair of pants. I just get a new pair.

There's a little song from when a guy was pretty mean to me, at least Guin thought so. She wrote the song and it goes like this:

> **When people die, I do not cry.**
> **When old friends turn, sadness reigns,**
> **But not for long, for joy is the natural state.**

And it is the natural state! The Master Jesus said, "My joy no man taketh from me." [17] It's weird. I'm reading hunks to you from books. I'm talking to you about other things. But all the time I know that with some of you the petals of the *Heart Lotus* are opening just a little bit.

There is no doubt that you have heard better things said by more literate individuals, but regardless of that, I'm doing a switch on you and I'm coming at you in a little different direction. Maybe it'll shake you a little bit so that all of a sudden, Wow! You'll say, "What's all this about? 'I AM,' right now! I can feel it inside of me." Careful, Miller, careful . . . .

Life, the Great Opera

How much have you investigated into the life that you have, into that which is functioning through you? This is very important! It's more important than all the rest of it, and yet we run out to somebody else to get some phoney answers that don't fit with us individually. We all have our own ideas, as well as things we want to have. And you're not going to be happy unless you get some of the things you really want. But if you are looking for that something which is **within you**, and **dig** what the trouble is all about (in other words, why you're having the particular difficulty that you are suffering through at this time)—well, who do you think could advise you better than your own SELF?

You've got to figure out your own troubles and work on them. Nobody else is going to do it for you. You have to come to it yourself. Now look, I'm not going into psychology, **I'm speaking of feelings as we humans feel them. It's not some set idea. You have to find that reality within you! Find it and BE there. The gentle stuff isn't gonna do it. You gotta have guts to do it, to make up your mind to really LOOK at things, at your own viewpoints, at your own biases and say, "Now look, old Biaso, get the hell off of there and let me take a look at it."** You've got the equipment to do it.

I'm going to say some things that might make you think I'm a bit off my rocker, but I'm not. I've lived a hell of a lot longer than most of you. So I know most of the things that we can hide from ourselves and just say, "Oh no, not that, not that." **YOU'RE LYING, TELL YOURSELF THE TRUTH.** What's causing you your difficulty? You have the **power** within you to find out whatever particular reality you could bring forward to help you in your particular place and do the things you want to do.

When you get into that place in your mind and you want to *think* about it, just forget who you are and what you are and resolve within your own consciousness the feeling of the One. Know that pure heart comes from your own inner being. Mind is something you use one time and another time and then you forget about it. **I'm trying to tell people that we all have it now and I know we've got it now, otherwise we wouldn't be alive! Being alive gets you a seat at the Great Opera. Eternity is a fact.**

Of course, a lot of folks don't believe that. They would say, "Oh well, what the hell, I'm going to die and be a batch of ashes and that's it." Yeah? Now that's very interesting. What do you think the ashes are? Where do they come from? What is it that giveth life to begin with? Nobody can explain life except you, for yourself, to yourself and within yourself.

If you don't like some of the other opinions about having another life, go ahead, but you'll have reincarnation, whether you like it or not. Maybe you'll have a few incarnations that are a little rugged on you, but you'll learn. They've got the thing set up that way. You're going to get it, whether you like it or not.

Spring

We've just had the spring equinox. In the spring, a young man's fancy turns to you know what . . . . So whadya gonna do about love?

Oh well, let's get into the spring thing first. There's a book called *As The Sun Moves Northward* written by Mabel Collins a number of years ago and it states that the spring equinox is the turning over of life, at least for the northern part of this planet. And that the spring equinox together with the summer solstice mark the period of the year in which to plant things and bring them to birth. And that the latter two, the autumn equinox and winter solstice, mark the time in which you would be getting the harvest, reaping whatever you deserve out of the year.

Maybe it's strange, but every year the equinox comes at the same time and every year those seeds come up out of the ground at the same time. We've all got ideas and we're going to plant and *we're going to do some wonderful things*. But we usually say it on New Year's and forget it the day afterward. Oh, you know, *we're going to work on it*, see, and then we plant the seeds of our endeavors. But when they don't come up right away, instead of giving them time, we reach in there and take them out to see if they're growing. That's no good. **A seed can't sprout until it rots! You've got to give everything that's in it, and then work on it.** What an idiotic thing—an old man like me talking about spring . . . .

I wanna tell you that the most beaten, misshapen thing in most people's lives turns out to be love. Because of their view of what love is. Now suppose I were to ask people in this room, "What is love?" I would get as many different versions as there are people in the room.

If real love is there, the lust is there, yes. But when the lust isn't there, when the newness wears off, you still see the thing that you love in the character of the other, you still *feel* it there inside of them. Love can't be thought, anyway. You've got to *feel* it. If you don't feel it, you're missing the biggest thing in the world. That is the essence.

We're using these vehicles, yes and they are marvelously crafted vehicles. But there is a whole other side of life that we are not looking at. You might think, "Well, what the hell, I've made a million bucks, I'm loaded, I'm enjoying myself, I'm enjoying everything in life even if I did cheat a few people and rob a few more." But this ain't the finish. We go after this, you see, and from the other standpoint, the idea is to find this ideal love and make it so great that you'll feel that way toward everybody. **Keep the lower part of the mind quiet enough, and long enough, to let the higher part speak to you.**

Everything you see here at this level is a projection, a mental concept, and you've got to make all those mental concepts **BE QUIET** so that you can feel that love **SURGE** up within you. And that's not limited to sentimentality. **It's a feeling of love for all of life!** Get out there under the stars on a dark night out in the country and look up at those hunks up there that are flashing and sparkling. You're all part of that. That's all a part of the thing that makes you click.

After all, when you get to the place where you're a human being, you've gone far enough in your education that you will carry on into it. **There is something inside of you, that spark, that animation, that consciousness that you can't ever soil.** That part is always pure, and there's another chance for everybody regardless of what they do. This is a school, we're going through karmic things, we get **WHACKED** here and there, so we'll learn something.

You've got to realize your at-one-ment with the All, and that the All is what's making it work. Now a simple way to do this without contemplating your navel or throwing yourself out of joint by holding some odd position is just to sit down sometime when you feel kind of quiet. Don't think about the past, but don't forget it either—it comes in handy, keeps you from stubbing your toe in the future—and don't think about the future because it isn't here yet. Look at the present as always moving and changing. **You** are capable of observing this, of understanding it, so therefore you can touch the hem of the garment right there! Watch the world going by—not tied by your hang-ups of the past or those of the future—just *feel* it, and if the feeling comes from the heart, you'll be filled with **ecstasy**, you'll feel yourself lifted out of your body.

You can't make this happen, it has to happen from inside. When the outside of your being has matured, the higher part of your own self speaks to you.

The Mind in the Head Is Just an Outpost

I have reached a point now where I can feel and think and have the feeling and thinking married. That's where it's at. Know that other people are you and you are them. When you talk to them, look 'em in the eye and reach into that depth of being that combines both mind and heart.

The mind in the head is just an outpost of THE MIND within your heart—where all your feelings are. During incarnation while we're learning the lessons, we learn to fall awake—I don't know what the hell they put us to work at then, but they'll figure out something. Our Oneness is scattered through the vehicle. The heart, the head, and the whole thing is one composite, synthesized reality. We're scattering it out to learn about it, so we can direct it and handle it better. [18]

That's one of the things this outfit Theosophy was put together for, to help people understand. It's really an underground movement, because it's opposed to so many hang-ups people have in their minds. It's a feeling of love and understanding. I don't mean the love that you have to possess everyone of the opposite sex that you desire. It would kill you in time . . .

See, I wear this phoney looking little medallion here that is supposed to be symbolic of the double Vajra. The double Vajra symbol is for this purpose: you can take the essence of what comes from that sex-force and lift it to your heart, and you can take the phoney ideas that you never figure out and drop them into your heart, and you can come into the higher consciousness which includes it all. Then whoever you meet, when you look into their eyes and they look into your eyes, you can feel your at-one-ment with them and their at-one-ment with you.

That's like a habit that the Sufis got—hugging everybody. The idea is meeting each other from HEART to HEART. I'm not looking for anything else, I just want to greet you as a fellow soul on this trip we're taking.

Each one of us is a microcosmic reflection of the macrocosm. In other words, within each one is a replica of everything that is contained in the solar system. All of the answers are within you. You have to find them by looking and inquiring into yourself.

We're Not Pushing Any Religion

Each great religion has its way to go, but ours is this: we're not pushing a religion, we're pushing **compassion**. That's the one thing that they can't dangle out there and say, "Well, there you are, that's the love!" Oh, yeah? It's invisible, you can't see it. And it's not only within us. **How do you think this whole thing is happening if it isn't a production of that ONE? It's not only a global Force, it's an ETERNAL FORCE.**

We learn the lessons of the physical vehicle: we get married if that's our particular way; we have children; they grow up and go. Maybe we take up another course of study or say, "Well look, I think I can live on my pension." Unless, of course, they established the pension so damn many years before that it's only small change now. **The real love, the deeper love that you feel between man and woman, that love in essence is unconditioned love. We live and move and have our being within that love . . . .**

All you have to do is **be** that and **live**. Live your life so that you don't hurt inside, in your own consciousness. Live your life so that you can live with yourself and be happy. And whatever of work one may be doing in life, or not being able to do, live within. Be contented in knowing that you *are* eternal and that this particular purpose and your own evolution are moving along. We all have responsibilities. We know what they are. We know where we are.

So many ideas that you have as young persons, in another thirty years, you'll have all different kinds of ideas running around in your head. But find that CENTER within you from which you can live a CONTENTED life in the LAP of ETERNITY and KNOW that the THATNESS that you are CANNOT BE DESTROYED ever.

Earthquake!

I imagine that everyone in this room had some kind of experience during the earthquake we went through a couple of weeks ago. I want to talk to you about the effect of the earthquake on the entire area, how it made everybody **think** and **feel** and then try to **do** something. That's what we're made up of—thinking, feeling, and doing.

For that moment, when it was **SHAKING** and you **FELT** it and you didn't know whether or not it was your last time on Earth, you wondered all of a sudden, "What religion did I belong to? Geez, I gotta have something going for myself. I may be going to hell in a basket."

Well, that's one way to look at it. Another way to look at it is for you to realize in your own minds that nothing in your lives is any more substantial than the very earth you're living on. **In that instant, everyone's mind was cleared of everything but FEAR,** "Where can I find a doorway and send one to me quick!"

Let the realization seep into your consciousness. So many people were having that experience at the same time, it has caused one of the biggest hangovers we've ever had in this city in my time. People say, "Oh well, I don't know, I can't sleep well, and these aftershocks are getting me."

Realize that there is nothing in your head, in your pocket, on your body or in your house that is permanent. But you didn't know at that moment that there is something INSIDE of you—the I AM said, "What am I going to do with that part of me? What am I going to do?" The body could disappear, but still you were, there was no argument about it. You felt it. You were being it. That's the important thing. Whether it was from fear or whatever, you knew that you wanted to save that precious thing that was **YOU**, not the you alone of the outer part, but that other part, you didn't want anything to happen to it. But you identified that other part with your body, "I don't want anything to happen to this body."

The real you that you were trying to save, that's the point you've got to get to FALL AWAKE, to know that there is THAT within this physical vehicle that no earthquake, no storm, no cyclone, no flood can destroy. That was never born and never dies, that's a SPARK of INFINITY, that is a part of God Himself! Whether you call it Christ or Allah or Buddha,

you are a part that now—not in some future! You're alive aren't you? You're breathing, aren't you? We all have that within us, and it will always sustain us.

At the moment of the earthquake, who were we thinking of? Do you know who everybody was thinking of? Themselves, of course. Hell, you didn't want to end up in the sewer someplace. On the other hand, if this city could live up to the compassion that it showed in the donations to the Red Cross, the Salvation Army, and other institutions for earthquake relief. For that moment, we all realized that the money we had wasn't worth a damn anyway. It might just be so much paper tomorrow . . . .But we all felt pure love inside, even in the love of keeping our own bodies. That love was FOR REAL.

Each person recognized just a little what I see when looking in your eyes—I can see me and I know that you're inside of me as well. We all are one. We all are of the spirit. We took this journey in incarnation to learn certain things. There isn't anyone in this area right now that hasn't lived thousands of lives. If you hadn't lived that many times, you wouldn't have the sense to know that there was something called reincarnation.

There is something inside of everyone of us, if we would just become aware of it, that is eternal. Now, you don't have to live a mambi-pambi life because something in you is eternal. You each have something that you have developed up to this point, with which you can help those around you—in understanding or whatever it may be or just in the feeling inside of you that you are ONE with all of them!

Be Who You Are

I'm going to talk at random. I always do. Because it is the only way I seem to be able to talk. I sort of throw everything to the wind and try to take it from the intuition and pure love.

Pure love is the main thing. Love without the possessiveness. Can you feel that love? Can you touch that impersonal, yet highly personal love? You can't be impersonal unless you're personal! And when you're personal, you're impersonal. Because when you're stingy, you're trying to keep it all for yourself. You don't have to do that. It's got to be universal love. **Sooner or later, we'll all realize the whole world is one family, one beautiful family.** That's the wonderful part of life.

If you don't shut off the thoughts that you have running wild in your mind, you can't meditate and you can't be at peace with yourself.

Now there are other times when you touch this MIND, suppose you go to the theatre and you hear music that's so wonderful that it lifts you right out of yourself. You ain't even thinking of who you are, you've become drunk on the music and you are right into the music and it's beautiful. That's what we want, the BEAUTY, the HARMONY within.

Another time your lower mind will shut off is when someone WHACKS you unexpectedly. They utilize that a lot in Zen. Then, for a minute, the guy has clearness of MIND. "What did ya hit me for?" He's there, he don't know it but he has turned this thinking off. Then, if he wished, he could turn to the heart and the heart would tell him something.

Or, another example, let's say you go to a show and you really get tickled. You start laughing, then the jokes get better and you're going, "WOW! Hilarious." Well, when you're at the top of your laughter, are you thinking about anything?

Can you just turn it off? Try it sometime. Turn off your thinking. Usually, you can't turn it off. You say, "It just keeps on going." Well, it does keep on going, if you let it. But the programmer for your computer is in the heart, and you can turn off all that software anytime you want. You're the only one who can do it.

BE WHO YOU ARE. Be. Feel your at-oneness with that I AM within you.

It's not something that you can get if you go someplace where someone says, "Well, if you lay down fifteen dollars and you stay here for a couple of weeks, I'll teach it to you." They can't. Nobody but you can bring you out of it. **This is part of the New Age! You're not going out to temples of religions of the past, you're going into the temple of the Living GOD—yourself!** We are all Gods in the making.

I say these things to people. Why? Not because you'll dig it now. The chances are ten to one that you'll say, "Oh, that crazy old coot with the fuzzy muff don't mean anything." But sometime when you are in a bind, maybe five years from now, maybe ten years from now, you'll reach back inside and that'll pop out. I'm placing it in your computers for that purpose, to use when needed.

We've all met before or we wouldn't be here now. We wouldn't be here in this room together. There wouldn't be enough people to come up and fill this room and listen to me if there wasn't some connection. All I'm trying to do is give you the benefit of what I have dug in this life.

You've read this and you've read that and you've read the other, but you have to have an experience before it's *real* to you.

We're probably living in the most materialistic time the world has ever known—everything is only measured by the THINGS that are here. But we're not our bodies, our lower minds or our feelings, we're not that. We are sparks of Immortality, something that you can't describe. You can give an idea of what happens with it, but you can't show a picture of it. And you don't see it when you come to it. You just feel such a vast relief that, "Ah, this is what I have been looking for all my life," that **peace that passeth all understanding.**

I know I'm NOTHING, no-thing, no-thing, not me, not me. I'm just a wild-assed spark of the Infinite functioning in the Finite! I can turn it on or turn it off any damn time I want to. I could drag you through a pool of sad-sack stories and have you crying tears as big as horse-turds. This is the magic that each one of us has within us.

My viewpoint is that you surrender yourself to your deeper spiritual SELF. And BE that spiritual SELF. BE WHO YOU ARE. And that's who you are! **You're all GOD.** You're carrying around the GENERATOR of FORCE within you. Use it. That's what you got it for. You just needed some silly-billy like me to come along and mention it to you.

It doesn't matter if I ever see any of you people again, you won't forget that reality within you. Because you haven't heard this from a famous minister that's a member of the *Hierarchy*, I'm just a jerk . . . .

Thus Spake Ramana

Did you know that we don't believe in any dogma or creed? The Theosophical Society is eclectic. We believe each great religion has the answer in it, and that through any of the great religions you can find it. But it's sort of thinned out a bit. Because when the theologians got a hold of the original teachings they did a bit of ad-libbing. In fact, they wrote volumes upon volumes about, about, about! They were very cagey about the nitty-gritty. They kept the nitty-gritty rather concealed. What we're trying to do here in the Society, in this particular lodge, is give you the very ESSENCE of something practical that you can use for the purpose of getting to the very same point that every religion is directing you toward.

People use to go to Ramana Maharshi and say, "Well, what do I do? How do I meditate?" And he would reply, "Ask the question, **Who am I?**" Don't do it like a mantra, with constant repetition ending nowhere, in smoke. Inquire into yourself as to who is the real I within you. Who is that? Where does it come from?

You've got to discount your body, your senses. What's the Real I, the center or essence of the intelligence as well as the emotions and the physical figure? Where does it come from? Find that point within you. And that's the point you need to pay attention to.

Now all of us are conditioned by our families, by our religion, our nationality, the particular country we came from, what we think of it, how we admire or don't admire it; we've got our biases and oppositions within our consciousness. But the CONSCIOUSNESS in itself, in its purity, doesn't have any biases. You can see the whole thing clearly. This is a way out, if you'll use it, a way out of the limitations of your personality and to finding the reality of who you really are inside of you.

Ramana never moved away from the place he lived. He was never important. He never talked in front of crowds of thousands of people. His ashram was called "the Wilderness Ashram." Ramana never had any guru or teacher. He got it from within himself. And I'm of the opinion that if any of us even get a touch of it, a smell of it, we've got to do it for ourselves. Nobody can do it for you. No one can tap you on the head or dunk you three times in a bucket of water and then you come out enlightened. That ain't gonna work.

We've got to get rid of the crap we have in our own noggins ourselves. We've got to realize that the mind is something we use, but the higher consciousness is in the heart, in the center of the heart. Knowledge is on one side of it, on the other are the realistic things of life. And when you're hooked with affairs of the heart that dampen our personality, bring it to a higher stage or get rid of it! Now I'm not talking against sex . . . .In Indian philosophy, concerning the essence, there are three phases: **SAT, CHIT and ANANDA. SAT** is being, **CHIT** is consciousness and **ANANDA** is joy or bliss. And that joy that even the four-footed animals and fish and insects enjoy as sex is the highest they can reach to find their BLISS. And that bliss is probably the highest bliss in your life that you'll ever have.

But when you have the aforesaid bliss, what are you thinking about? You're not thinking about the other person, you're not thinking about a damn thing, you're floating in ecstasy. Huh? Your mind is absolutely clear there. But you can't have a number of people around just giving you sex so that you can get to that clear place. There's got to be a better method than that. Of course, I know a lot of teenagers who have damned near killed themselves trying. But they usually end up standing very seriously before some minister and soon thereafter start educating a child for eighteen years.

But there is that same ecstasy within you that you can feel with *a gentle, in-drawn breath*, if you're radiating out universal love at the same time. **We're a multitudinous expression of one clear Force of Reality, and we've got to tune in to it to get back to where we started from.** Maybe you say, "What's the wisdom aspect, what are all those things we have to remember and put down in a book? And what about all those thousands of libraries we never get a chance to go through?" The wisdom aspect is pure, unselfish love within. Impersonal, unselfish love.

Can you stop thinking? How many of you can stop thinking regardless of whatever kind of meditation you've been given without fixating on a particular point? Just stop! In another words, there's a guy swinging his arm. If he decides he wants to stop swinging his arm, he stops. Why can't you do that with your consciousness?

So most of them say worship something, worship this, that, or the other and that will do it for you. Well, this guy Ramana Maharshi had a different idea—he said, "Use self-inquiry." Inquire into the thoughts you have. What do they amount to? And then, look into all of reality and realize that we are ruled by dualism, by the opposite ends of each thing.

Another thing to remember is that whatever happens to you—and it isn't all pleasant—learn to accept it if you can't change it. If you can change it, go ahead and change it. If you can't, accept it. Live with it and find out what you can find out from it.

We have social structures and we gotta live by them to keep the world stuck together—that's good. But this is a private inquiry on the part of yourselves. You want to wake up that part of you, so that you each individually can do something about it. If you come to more awareness, it isn't going to be somebody else who gave it to you, it's going to be by your own attitude change; a change in your viewpoint, in how you look at it.

You know I could build you all kinds of pictures of imaginary places up in the sky and out in the universe, but you don't need anymore soft tapes in your head. You need to come around to who you are, and you are that REALITY within.

Even in ancient Egyptian philosophy, they said, "Realize that you as an individual are a microcosmic reflection of the macrocosm." So the whole universe is reflected within you, you're a prism through which it shows. You can make that light shining. But if the light's turned off, it's just a hunk of glass. There's no beauty.

Love, light and life. And the light of your body—if you don't breathe, you're not going to be using that body. That don't mean that you die. **You were never born.** Each one of you are a creation of the ONE. As Jesus said, "Call no man thy Father." You're of God or the ONE. It's not sacrilege, it's just the goofy stuff I believe in. You can use it or not use it as you wish.

You can not use it and say, "Well, that guy's illiterate, he doesn't know anything; he hasn't any intellectual background; he hasn't gone to any good schools; he's a nobody." But, you know, you're all nobodies. You are no body. You are that life within it that brings it to life. You are that SPARK.

When you **FALL AWAKE** to the REALITY, you realize that it's all ONE and you realize that it was all for the purpose of educating you to a certain place so that you could find your way back home. But, in one sense, you've never left that home, because **IT** is what **VIVIFIES** you **NOW.**

The Biggest Problem We Have in the World

The biggest problem we have in the world today is GREED.

Everybody wants to take what someone else has got. Then after they get what that somebody else has got, they look for some other somebody else's to take from them too. But they're never satisfied inside. They're never happy. They're never at peace.

You have to get at peace with yourself. That's why the old man, Ramana Maharshi, always said, "Ask yourself, **Who am I?**" Do it as an inquiry. Go through your senses. Go through your thinking. Go through your body. Who are you? Who is the I?

The Sufis point to the Heart. *The Siva Sutras* point to the heart. But we couldn't recognize that until we had gone through a lot of stuff that came from other parts of the world, because we were raised with it and were mad as hell with the dogma and creed that was laid on top of the truths that were given in Christianity.

Do you know how many people started out with Buddha when he decided to teach 'em? They were up in a little hut and there were six of them. And it is one of the biggest religions in the world. But it has its various phases and facets too, it has its dogmas and creeds.

We here in this century, particularly in this country, have religious freedom. It may be one of the only ones we have, but we do have that. So you find out. Ramana, before he died in the 1950's, brought an element that is not usually recommended, that of inquiry into yourselves. FIND THAT REALITY.

As far as your desires are concerned, they're normal and natural. But most people, after they accomplish a desire, even if it's a big one in their life, they're not satisfied. A guy says, "Geez, if I ever get $50,000, I'll coast for the rest of the way . . . ." He won't. He'll get the $50,000, invest it in something and then try to get more from somebody else. But when you've got enough to feed and clothe yourself, you can get a lot of living out of that if you can just find peace within.

Sure, you're ambitious for your children. And in this particular economy, you have to be ambitious for them. But you don't want them down there groveling in the dirt in front of you. Well, neither does the One itself want us groveling, it wants us reaching for the stars. Because we gotta grow, just as the flowers have to grow. But if you start messing up, trying to use a screwdriver to open up a rose, what would you get? Wouldn't be much of a rose, would it?

We're all in a garden. As Inayat Khan said, "The greatest Bible is Nature itself." What's growing within you? And who are you? Look inside. The outside world is pressing in on us. We have to meet it. But all the difficulties you have to face, in life, the concepts you have to face some your own, some those of other people, can you do it from that center of reality, knowing that you ARE and that all you have to do is BE?

You are really free inside to experience whatever you wish, to go wherever you wish; but, if you start extending your desires and not holding them down to a sensible view, remember, **DESIRES NEVER LIVE UP TO THEIR PROMISES.** They can't.

I'm sure you can recall thinking, "If I just had that . . . ," but as soon as that desire was fulfilled, you said, "Well, I'd like . . . " It's all right. But don't you see, you're chasing outward all the time. You're not looking deep inside to see what you can put out, what you can give. I'm taking a chance. I'm being a giver.

The truth can't be sold and can't be bought. And I don't believe it can be taught very well. But if they're around the one who's teaching them, sometimes they catch some of it. It can be caught. Because the words you say are not the way you convey truth. Truth is conveyed in pure Silence, without anybody trying to tell anybody else anything, and just by being AT-ONE.

It's closer than your hands and feet, closer than your jugular vein. It's your heart. It's the love within. And anything that goes in another direction sooner or later destroys itself.

Theosophy

One long word, Theosophy, which breaks down into *theos sophia*. which means God-wisdom in Greek. Theos, God the masculine. Sophia, the wisdom, the feminine. Theosophy has been in existence throughout eternity, but this particular outfit has been going since 1875.

When I talk to people here, I really talk to them more about themselves than anything else. And in talking about Theosophy, I'm really talking to each of you individually. Each of you have that spark of eternity that was never born and never dies within you. Each one of us in this room is eternal. Now you might say, "If I'm eternal and I've lived a number of incarnations, why don't I remember them?" That's one of the first things that comes up, because most folks in Theosophy do believe in reincarnation.

Without the principle of reincarnation, or of being reborn, there wouldn't seem to be any fairness in the ways things are dished out to people. Some people are born with a golden spoon in their mouths, others with a shovel full of coal; some with good bodies, others with bad bodies. Looked at over a number of centuries and incarnations, we could see where things were being worked out and different capacities were being developed in different people. And a handicap means that the higher part of yourself decided that you were in good enough shape to meet that and carry it and work through it to find out about it.

Another thing, we don't try to reach into your pocket for money. We're not commercial. It's one of the only organizations that I know of in the non-profit field that isn't a religion and has endured since 1875.

The motto under our symbol out there on the wall says, "There is no religion higher than Truth." Of course, we in this particular lodge have added another line to that, "And no power greater than love." Because love is what makes it all go around. **That's what Theosophy is all about — wisdom and love. There is a place in *The Secret Doctrine* where it states very clearly that Theosophy isn't the "love of wisdom," but rather "the wisdom of love."** If each one of you thinks back over your life, you will see that it is always feeling that moves you, the feeling of love.

Now there are those who are ambitious and figure that someday they're going to be able to do a lot of magical things like the things they read in a flock of books. Maybe they will. But it will be a hell of a long time. It takes time to learn about these things. You don't learn them in your mind. It's when you come to the reality itself and start feeling it and living it. It's when you turn out to be givers and not takers.

Sure, I've done a lot of learning. I've whacked my head against the wall a few times until I realized that this illusion was fairly solid if I try to get through it in that manner. It won't work.

As you live, even in this lifetime, so will you reap. If you're a giver, not a taker, there will always be more for you to give. But what you're giving in one form or another by helping someone else is a form of pure love coming from that inside of you. We're never out of pure love, we're never out of the love that takes us to that higher ecstasy and helps us to expand our consciousness to a content with which it can comprehend all of it, but still live by the spirit within.

If you come up here and ask to join the lodge, they'll tell you, "Well, hang around for awhile and see whether you like what we are doing. If you don't, forget about it." And you don't have to join anyway, you can go to everything we're putting out. We don't have any members-only meetings.

Each person has to find that reality for themselves. Hell, if I can do it, any of you can do it. I'm nobody. I don't have any titles hanging out of my cars. I don't belong to any *hierarchy*. **THE ONLY HIERARCHY THERE IS, IS REALITY!** That's the very Oneness itself. And we *all* belong to that. Each one of us is IMMORTAL.

If you're interested in Theosophy, we've got a couple of rooms full of books back there on any subject you can imagine, in all phases of so-called occultism, pseudo-occultism, some genuine stuff. But you don't need to read those books. You've got it inside of you, if you'll just feel for it and let your consciousness expand to a point where you can understand it. Each and every one of us has that. It's a built-in feature. That's our own do-it-yourself kit. But if you're so tied-up with the ideas that have been packed into your head since you were born and what you brought over with you from prior incarnations, maybe you wouldn't think of it. If you could just BE STILL FOR EVEN FIVE MINUTES, you'd find that you're feel-thinking things from your own heart, that's telling you where you are and what you can do to straighten it out.

We wanted the particular bodies we're wearing. Otherwise, we wouldn't be here. We started this job a long time ago, as immortal sparks of eternity, to go through this school, to learn it. Regardless of how many times we had to come back.

There is no special time when everyone will all of a sudden have the realization or start living it. It's up to each one of us. That's the wonderful thing about it. You've got FREE WILL. You pick the time when you are to come to enlightenment. You pick the time where you're gonna find the particular thing. You have picked it inside, deep within your own heart. So be still, and go in there.

They say we're coming into a New Age. Well look, we've got people from all different levels here now. But some of those are beyond the place where we are, *in the world but not of it*. They tell you what they think that you can take at the particular place that you're in. But there is no limit on the advancement that you can make, if you go to the source within you and follow what it says to you. But it don't SAY it, it gives you a FEELING.

Right now, in this room, is probably the future controller of a planet out in some solar system. Because Planet Earth, the one on whose body we're living, was once even as you and I.

And if you pay much attention to what I say, YOU'RE NUTS! But if you get what I'm trying to give you from my heart, there's no limit to that. That's the kind of love that I just want to give out all the time. And it goes out, and it never empties. Because it's drawing on the source itself.

If you come into the lodge and decide you want to hang around and you say, "Look, I'd liked to be a member . . . ," just remember: you don't have anybody to lean on. We don't use any leaners at all in the outfit. There's nobody to lean on. Sure, they'll talk to you. We don't want someone talking down to people either. All I'm doing is throwing out ideas. Some of what I've dug myself in my lifetime. I wanna share it with you.

When we have someone give a Friday night talk, we let the person talk for about fifteen minutes, then we get on his tail and tell him all about it. Not out of viciousness. But just throwing questions. Expressing our own ideas about what he had to say. That's the way it is. We're a bunch of rebels that come to this place. And I'm gonna keep it that way. After all, this country was founded by rebels. They weren't satisfied in any other country, so they took off for themselves.

The Theosophical Society used to have an "Esoteric School." But in this lodge, we don't have it anymore. Because we talk about the *esoteric* in open meetings. What was *esoteric* at one time is no longer *esoteric*. They're things we use in conversation. It's expanding. Consciousness must always expand. The point is to have a place to stand during that expansion and that place is within you, in the Clear Light.

What Do You Want Out of Life?

What do you want out of life? Nine of ten people don't know what they want. They haven't figured out a goal for themselves.

If you do figure out a goal, then see if you have the capacity in your physical, mental, emotional make-up to do it. If you have, then go for it. Nine out of ten times, you'll make it.

But if you don't have the physical capacity or intelligence or emotions to do the job, then pick something else that's in the neighborhood of it. But have some direction to go in.

The truth of the matter is if you'll just be still, be very still, that which is within you will tell you what you should do this time. It's a personal thing that you individually work out.

Nobody can say, "Well, you'd be a good . . . ." That's a lot of hooey.

This Too Shall Pass

When you see the terrible things that are happening in the world, particularly in the Middle East right now, just remember, "*This too shall pass.*"

A great king wanted a word of advice, something that would work for him when he was prosperous or when he was having a tough time, or whether he felt sorrow or happiness. So this old guy said to him, "There's just one answer to it — *this too shall pass.*"

We live in a world of duality, man and woman, up and down, in and out, right and wrong. But it's really a Oneness. And although we live in a world of duality, we can come to the Oneness, that spark within each one of us and can take everything that happens with equilibrium.

If the situation demands action on your part, take the action. But don't let it disturb that point within you which is always at peace, always in harmony, always in equilibrium. With it, you are free to move in any and all directions. It's all-enveloping, all-understanding. You've got it.

You touched it for a minute when you were doing the healing circle, that beautiful ritual you were doing just now. Ritual can bring it to you. Know that within you, *with just a gentle, in-drawn breath* and no thought, and the feeling of the love of God flowing out, you can have that peace and ecstasy that lifts you out of yourself.

Most people are trapped by sex and they think that's the end of it. But there is that which you can have happen within your very being, not in some other lifetime, not a thousand years from now, but **NOW!**

When it happens, you can just feel yourself to be a bright light, whether they can see it or not, and it's flowing out to them. When you feel that, you have become one with the reality that you truly are.

If Anyone Comes to You for Help

If anyone comes to you for help, let them talk to you, because you can't find out where they're at unless they talk to you. You're just guessing at it otherwise. By using your own intuition, you can jump to it, yes. But even to get to that, you should let them talk to you. And in their talking to you, you'll touch that Oneness inside of them. Then you can help them, if you, in turn, can just have an open heart with the love of God flowing out.

I don't care if the person's a murderer or a thief on dope, they're a part of you. You got to remember that. **I'll try to bring it to your consciousness in rather a coarse way, but it'll give you the idea: I don't know any of you men who would care to put your testes on a block of wood and hit 'em with a hammer, and I don't know any of you ladies that would like to run one of your breasts through a ringer.**

Think it over. **Every time you hurt someone else, you're hurting yourself.** Maybe that vulgar down to earth thought will STOP you when you feel like tearing somebody up even verbally. That don't do any good. You're only hurting yourself. Many times it comes back at you quickly.

If you can't say anything good about someone, don't say anything.

You Don't Need to Worry
About the Coming of the New Age

You don't need to worry about the Coming of the New Age. It's just your job to find the SELF. Call it Allah or Christ or Buddha or whatever. That's the reality within you, that's who you really are. That's why my view on religions is rather eclectic. Because I realize that all of them of any importance are teaching one thing, and it comes in four letters—LOVE.

Each teacher of humanity, each one of the great ones, came to a particular ethnic group. But the guys who came afterwards built up a lot of dogma and creed about it; they were just taking you away from letting you center on that reality that you are.

Your job is to become truly the universal. It's there. It's within you. You'll feel it.

Nothing

My subject is *NOTHING*. Let us look at what I mean by *NOTHING*.

Everything of a spiritual nature, by the scientific community is considered *NOTHING*. Because there is no factual, actual proof for it. So we really have been talking about *NOTHING* ever since we've been established here at the lodge and since the founding of the Theosophical Society, as far as the intellectual look at things is concerned.

I want to give you a little touch, a few little points about it.

I did a very unforgivable thing. I went to a guy's talk and he said, "Well, anybody who wants to say something, go ahead and say it." Now I didn't say anything.

But someone behind me said, "I got a wife and two kids, and I'd like to know how I can get to that place of Clearness, that Voidness, that light . . . " and he kept on talking. I stood it for so long and then something went off inside, and I said, "Why don't you realize you're *NOTHING* and then you'll understand **EVERYTHING!**"

This is true if you can get your *EGO* out of the way, so that you can realize that you're the *NOTHING* that I am speaking of, that spiritual REALITY. Then you'll know what it is all about. You won't have to read any books about it. Your very inner consciousness will expand and you will KNOW what it's all about. After all, the consciousness itself, the higher mind itself, is located here, inside the chest. As Sufis we call it heart. The higher mind is located in the heart.

Once you get into the higher mind, or *turiya* state, the Clear state, the heart opens up for you. It opens up as fast as you want it to. But it is up to you individually and what I'm talking about is *NOTHING*.

How many of you were on the bridge? A number of you, okay. There were 800,000 people on the bridge. Where did they come from? Who told them to be there? Who said they were going to win anything by being there? Nobody, nobody at all.

So when this *NOTHING* is so big that it can move that many people to do something that they probably didn't ever know why they did it except to be there, that's wonderful! Because in their minds, anybody that would tell them to get up that early in the morning, they would say, "You're nuts.

We don't get any chance to win anything. What the hell are we going there for? Let's stay in bed or watch it on TV." Of course, being lazy, I watched it on TV. It was wonderful.

They even flattened out the bridge. You can't put enough trucks and cars on it to do that . . . I'll tell you another thing about it, it so happens that a number of psychiatrists that specialize in suicide were having a convention here in the city and they all said, "Well, look, if you do that and have all these people on the bridge, at least forty or fifty of them will jump off." Nobody jumped off. There were even little kids walking on the catwalks outside the railing and nothing happened to any of them.

Stop and think about it! If one politician in this city could get that many votes, he'd be running for president right now. 800,000 is more than our basic population of the city.

But remember that's a bridge, a bridge on the Golden Gate. Something inside them told them something, and maybe that something that hasn't come clear to them goes something like this:

> **Only through the orchid door of the heart**
> **And the violet flame therein,**
> **Can you place your feet on the rainbow bridge**
> **That leads to the city of the Golden Gate**
> **And the shrine of Clear Light therein.**

Stop and think about that for a minute. Nobody said anything to them about anything like that but they felt the pull. Are you still gonna try to tell me that *NOTHING* don't mean something? Think about it.

The city hired a guy from L.A. to give us an idea of how many people were going to be on the bridge and paid him $20,000. He said 150,000 to 200,000. He got twenty grand for that! Nobody guessed it right. Because something moved the hearts of 800,000.

So from now on never tell me that *NOTHING* can't move things. That *NOTHING* was something in their hearts, something they realized as part of their nature, an ideal. They thought, "This is the Golden Gate Bridge, it's the most wonderful thing of its kind in the world," and they went there. But it was their hearts speaking to them, and they probably didn't know why.

There is more in *NOTHING* than you think. Well, everything in life that we can think of is divided up into dualities anyhow. There is always a dual side to everything. There is a right-hand side of the brain and a left-hand side of the brain. The left-hand side is strictly intellectual. These people were moved from the other side, the right-hand side. They weren't moved by anything outside themselves either, they moved themselves from INSIDE. They knew that the Golden Gate Bridge took them to the City of the Golden Gate. They knew that reality. It hit 'em and it hit 'em from *NOTHING*. Explain it? You can't.

I hope WHOEVER made those 800,000 people show up on the bridge pokes a little some of this into 'em. WOW! Wouldn't it be wonderful? But, you know, when you decide to go into mysticism or anything of an inner, higher nature and you say, "I'm gonna make this happen, I'm going to come to realization," it doesn't work. **You can't make it happen. You've got to let it happen.**

Making it happen would be the same thing as if you had a flower bud, a rose bud, and said, "Gee, I'd like to have a full rose, I'm not going to wait for nature to open this rose up." So you get yourself a screw driver and start opening it up. Well, it won't be much of a rose.

If you start realizing you're *NOTHING*, you'll catch the feel of it. At first, it might scare the Hell out of you. But keep trying. It won't do you any harm. Really, it won't hurt you a darn bit. In fact, after a bit, you're waiting for it. You hope it hits you again.

I don't know. Here I am trying to read something to you. I get so carried away by my own feelings, I want to put so much juice in it so you get something from it, that I start not even reading words right. It just shows how swept away you can be in the love of God, and the love of God is the love of people. Everyone is God. You've read the Bible: "Be Still and Know, I AM God."

You can be very still and *feel* for it, *feel* for that eternal feeling, then after you get a touch for that eternal feeling, *just feel this love* flowing out for everybody. Not holding on to it. I'm just letting it flow out to you.

It's a wonderful feeling, I assure you. You see, I'm nuts enough to try it, and I like it. So I think as long as I like it, I'll try to sell some other people on liking it.

I think you might be surprised. A lot of things might start happening that would surprise you very much. The trouble with most religions, many religions, is that there is so much superfluous stuff before you get to the snapper, the point of realizing that you're *NOTHING*

I'm trying to tell you how you can be *NOTHING*. I'll tell you another way, a quicker way. I'm sure the authorities wouldn't think this was very good. Another way to be *NOTHING* is to have a belly laugh.

Did you ever stop to think that when you really LAUGH, you're not thinking about a damn thing! You're perfectly clear. **All you gotta do is laugh.** So if it's all serious and they're having a big argument, if someone can pull a fast gaga and put a few belly laughs into it, everybody says, "Oh, to hell with it, we'll take care of that next month."

I'm trying to give you the nitty-gritty. I know I'm nuts for doing it. I should be charging at least $150.00 every time you come to see me. I can't do that.

Very early on, I realized that anything I say or do, I can't charge money for it. Because if I did, it wouldn't be for real. The minute you start charging something for it, you've shut off the deal, you've made it a business, as far as understanding the reality is concerned. I suppose if I had figured out a way to take people's money, I'd be fairly prosperous by now.

If you're having trouble with love and it's not working, give 'em more love, more love! That doesn't mean making slaves out of them, but a love that is a Oneness, that is eternal; that's you helping because you love everybody and they're a part of you and you're a part of them.

You don't want anyone to pay for saying that. **You want to feel it and BE it, and then it's for real.** I LOVE IT! I LOVE IT! So each time I try to do a rap it seems kind of silly or kind of whacky, but, I'm trying to tell you. Of course, I'm an idiot, I act like an idiot and I admit I'm crazy. If you find anything worthwhile, take it. It's yours. There's no charge. It's just friends. It's yours. It's the love of God.

Savoir-Faire

Savoir-Faire. You do know what it means, don't you? Anyone care to volunteer what it means? Savoir-Faire: know-how. And isn't that what we're all trying to get, know-how. To know how to handle ourselves so that we can make it to that point of FALLING AWAKE. That's what we're all trying for. *Savoir Faire*—being able to do everything the right way at the right time—what does it amount to? It amounts to mental and emotional equilibrium.

Now most of us don't care particularly about finding that equilibrium, for various reasons, emotionally because we usually have very tight fixations and mentally because we like to flip our lids now and then. Well, it's all right to flip your lid, but you've got to find a balance inside of you.

After all, we're composed of mind, emotions and body. As far as the way we usually deal with them, if mind is predominant, we might have a very cold-blooded individual, and if the emotions are predominant, we might have a very emotional individual. Sooner or later, we have to bring the emotion and mind into harmony. And remember, you got a body there too, so be kind to it. It's the only one you get for this particular trip, you'll have to wait till another trip before you get another body.

I got a little story to tell you about *savior-faire*. A number of years ago, I was married and working out at the Goman's Gay Nineties. I'd get home after 2:00 in the morning. When I'd get home naturally my wife—she was working for Standard Oil—had to be sleeping. So I opened the door and I thought, now I don't want to wake her up. I'll go quietly into the house and nothing will happen. She said from the bed, "Who is it?" I said "Joe," and she said, "Joe who?"

Now, my friends, there's where you need *SAVOIR FAIRE*. Right there! Are you gonna smack her? Are you gonna say, "Who's the other Joe?" Or get a gun and knock her off? I mean it's possible. Everyone has unexpected events—a time, place, condition—that they didn't expect to come up against.

For instance, I have a couple of people here tonight who have a great devotion for a certain teacher. If they find out that the teacher isn't playing square with the other people in their group, what do they do? What can they do? That's when you need savoir-faire. You look at it. If the teacher's given you something worthwhile and lifted you up, well and good. If the other part's there, it's there. You can't say anything about it. You can just hope that all of him will fall awake as wonderfully as that one part of the individual is.

It's a rough way to look at it though, because when someone does something unpleasant to us, nine times out of ten we want to whack him or kick him. But that isn't gonna do any good. There is only one thing that can do any good over the long run and that's *pure love*. And love, if it's of a universal nature, will take care of it **IF** you realize you love someone and you love them intensely, and beyond that, there's this other part of you where *savoir-faire* lives and that's universal in its attitude. **OTHERWISE**, you couldn't look at things and see them as clearly as you do. "**Breathing in and breathing out, That's what life is all about. You have lots of time to spin, breathing out and breathing in.**"

You have a potential within you. You are that certain life within. You haven't been here once, you've probably been here thousands of times, you're probably getting around to the place where you'll fall awake if you don't watch it. Then you'll say, "Jesus, did I spend all those centuries . . . .Yeah, I didn't need to do that. All I needed to realize was SAVOIR-FAIRE—the right thing at the right time!" Find the balance within yourself, within your own hearts, a place that is never disturbed, THAT point.

The Tibetans say the white bodhi-citta comes down from the top and the red bodhi-citta comes up from the bottom, and if you get it so they meet at the heart, then you're a high lama. Well, we're not high lamas, but we get some ideas. It works. It works. You can find Peace within. If you can make your mind still, you'd be in that place right in the moment. How many of us can make our minds still? If we're not talking to somebody else or listening to somebody else? All the time there's a conversation going on there of the things you want or the things you don't want, all the time. Why don't you let it be still and take a vacation?

Somebody asked me, and I told her but I took it from a terrible source. She said, "What do I do to get to that place?" I said, "**Sit still, shut up, and get out!**" One way to get beyond the lower mind is through love, light, and life. I don't care who you're married to or how happy you are, realize that there is a part of you that can expand that love to include everybody in the world.

Now here's what I'm going to use as an argument that you can do it: you can go outside and you've been busy with your affairs of the day, but if you look up at the sky, you can see all the planets, can't you? Of course, you know you're standing on this particular planet or at least you assume you are. You've got your feelings at a particular place in your emotional life. But that is only the lower grades of this part that you can enjoy even while you're there and then extend your love to include everyone. Try it. It's a great feeling.

Just feel love, and when you feel love, you'll just start BOOM! BOOM! BOOM! The stuff will start going on in your chest and you'll love it. Then you've stepped beyond this lower mind. But then, of course, you start thinking about something and it comes back awful quick. You say, "Yeah, I know but what am I going to do about this and how am I going to do that. What about clothes for the kids?" But that universal love can give you that *freedom* any time.

We, at this time, are coming around, or at least, getting in the neighborhood (a few hundred or thousand years) of the Aquarian Age. And in this Aquarian Age, you're going to be using the consciousness and when you start using the consciousness, you want to be able to figure things out for yourselves. A lot of people in this country want to figure things out for themselves. So try it. Nobody else can come and pat you on the head and give you a pair of wings. Honest, it doesn't work. You've got to do it for yourself, in yourself.

Say you are in a tight bind mentally and you don't know what to do about it. I've had any number of people come to me with difficulty they were going through in their consciousness and nine times out of ten they only saw a couple of sides of it, the positive and the negative. By just being still and looking at it as if it isn't you . . . my, my, my . . . you find out multitudinous ways that you can come back to the same thing and take care of it.

If I had any intentions of setting you up for a gimmick where I could milk you for your loot, I wouldn't have you come here, 'cause this ain't for it. We're not trying to get any tame pussycats to jump through circles for us. We're trying to help each individual FALL AWAKE for themselves.

Chances are ten to one, each one of you will do it in a different way, only applicable to you individually. Some people you can give a boot. Some people you can talk to, other people you've got to kick in the can. For some people, a book is enough, but other people, NO! They have got to wait till they hit a situation like, "Oh God, what am I going to do now? I haven't got this and I haven't got that. *Whatever will I do?*" Then you got to practice that thing, *savoir-faire*.

The hardest thing is when people come and ask for advice. What the hell, I'm kind of loose with giving advice. But I always tell 'em don't do what I tell you! You want a suggestion, I'll tell you something about it the way I see it. But each individual has to make their own decisions. If they don't make their own decisions, it isn't going to work out right. Because if they don't make their own decisions and you make them for 'em, and it's successful, then they'll always come back to you for more decisions. Well, the only thing is then they're leaning on you.

Another thing is that if you didn't have any scruples, you could be walking on them, and they wouldn't even know you were doing it. They'd think, "Well, that's fine as long as he settles everything." It ain't that way. It isn't that way!

You've gotta suggest the best suggestion you can give to 'em and then they go their own way. Of course, I don't know a damn thing about it. I'm not a psychiatrist or anything like that. In fact, I had someone jump on me not so long ago, and they said, "Well, you advise so and so and you advise so and so," and they said, "When are you going to put out your shingle?" I'm not going to put out any shingle. **Because I don't think the truth can be bought or the truth can be sold. To tell you the truth about it, I think it can only be CAUGHT! You hear enough of it going around, after a bit you say, "What the hell, I'll try it." It'll work out all right.**

But to just say, "Well, look, you just give me so much money and I'll tell you exactly what to do in your situation," to me, in my mind, that's phony. Nobody can know exactly what another person's situation is. Nobody can know exactly what another person is thinking, not only in their lower mind, but in their consciousness itself. Everybody has got to do it for themselves. No one can carry you piggy-back. It's within your own thinking, feeling, and living. That's where it's at!

So you might go to a Zen teacher and he might WHACK you over the head because he knows the proper time to WHACK you and that would bring you out of it. It's possible. It all depends on the individual, what your attraction is.

There is a central point that makes the whole thing hang together and work. Or have you ever examined inside of you to see what the central point of your functioning stems from within yourself? What makes you go and do the thing? Are you doing it particularly for money? Or is it desire for certain things you want to have? Why are you doing it? YOU have to dig in yourself and find it. Sure, you can go to a psychiatrist and have free association for fifteen years and at the end of the fifteen years, you ain't cured yet. You're still a good customer though. So find it yourself.

I listen to the TV and the radio, I listen to all the stuff they're trying to sell people for things they've got wrong with them that I never even heard of. I said to Guin, "Look, as long as you and I are in our eighties for Godsake, let's stay away from those doctors. They'll want to experiment on us to prove their method is best."

You know my method is going along pretty good now. I've gotten to eighty-three . . . .

I haven't any desire to die and I don't give a damn much whether I live except that I would miss all you beautiful people that come to see me, and that I saw on the walk for years. There is some kind of link between us, at least that I feel. Look, it isn't anything tangible. It isn't anything that you could say or sing or whistle or dance about, it's something inside; **you meet certain people and you just know!** Not any particular working of logic in the head, you're just aware. Call it intuition if you want to, but it happens.

We listen to that part of us all the time. Dogs, cats, and kids have that part working better than we have, they know who likes them and who don't. And boy, will they get away from you, if you don't like them. And if you do like them, they'll crawl all over you.

We have that within us. We know what we really want, if we'll just be still and look at it.

As far as desires, if we lived within our incomes, think of how it would ruin the credit card business. We have people who are making thirty, forty, fifty thousand dollars a year but don't have a pot to piss in or a window to throw it out of because they say, "Oh, I'll put a little more on this card. I'll put a little more on that card. Oh well, I got another card . . . ."

In the old days you couldn't go to a bank and get a credit card. You couldn't get credit unless you had something substantial or the banker himself really liked you. Then they'd say, "Here, okay, I believe you have the integrity and honesty to pay it back. I'll give you the money." But that day's gone.

The thing is, don't let yourself go broke within your own being, in your heart, in your own consciousness. Hold on to the real thing that you've got there. Don't let that be broken. That's the main thing. A person can get more money. They can get this or that or the other. They can get by. But don't give up on yourself. Know **THAT** within you that's immortal, was never born, and will never die. It's eternal.

Love, the Breath, and Just One Person to Another

If you weren't interested in love in its very essence you wouldn't be here. If you're looking for an alibi to sneak out of your present responsibility, forget it. I haven't got anything to say to help you do that. Love is pure love, but pure love is not trying to get anything, it's not trying to hold anybody exclusively. If the other person loves you and it's going out to you enough, and it's going out to her . . . . Love is a wonderful thing at the point where everybody meets it.

Whether to be married or not to be married, that is the question. Most men don't particularly want the responsibility of a family, so they run away from it up to a certain point where their foot slips and they can't help themselves. So if your foot hasn't slipped, you've been missing an awful lot. Because you have a chance to play the part of God to those little ones that you bring in, those egos that you bring in. Remember, they're not yours. You don't own them. You just happen to be a good vehicle for them to get here. Don't think that you keep them under your thumb all your life.

In the old days, I met many women beyond the middle age spot who said, "Well, I'm devoted to my mother." It was because their mothers kept them under their thumbs like that. You've all got your own lives to live.

Pure devotion is pure love. Devotion to whoever may be your idea of an anthropomorphic God—a human figure that walked on Earth and represents all the finest things you can conceive of in your consciousness. If you wish to make that person, that particular avatar, the one that you surrender to, that's wonderful. In Theosophy, you can surrender or not surrender. That's up to you.

Theosophy shows the way that by getting to your higher mind, by disciplining yourself in your thinking, you can get to the place and that's call *jnana*. I'm not speaking *jnani* tonight. I am speaking pure love. **Pure love will get you there! Even if it's love for a lesser individual than one of the great ones. Because the very purity of your love will purify your mind as well.**

If you take the mind trip, you've got to work with it gradually and bring it down. Sooner or later, you'll have both the mind and the heart. But the heart is the way that is offered to you by Sufism. If you can let your mind drop into your heart to the extent that you measure everything by the amount of pure love that's coming out of you, you're following the rule called ACCEPTANCE OF LIFE where you are. Accept what you are, and BE who you are and what you are!

We all say we're part of the One, but how do you know you're part of the One? How do you know it? You want me to give you a few scientific explanations to prove you're part of the One? Nobody I know of that is alive at this level can live without breath. We don't keep track of breaths we breathe during the night and day. We can assume that without the breath—and that breath is one of the places the word Brahman comes from—we're not here, this particular manifestation is eliminated.

Breathing in and breathing out. In the East they teach you that in your breathing in and out you can put yourself on a discipline, so that every breath you breathe in is on a **HA**, and what you breath out is a **SA**. **HAMSAH,** that's the famous bird that flies.

You should know that your breath influences your thinking. Nobody can stop breathing and think with any coherence for any great length of time. So when you're angry, slow down your breath; and when you slow down your breath to a normal breathing, you're not angry anymore. You say what did I do that silly thing for, I don't have to be mad. Next time you get real mad, put your hand on your chest and see how you feel. Hyperventilating is what they call it in the medical profession, I believe, when you're breathing real fast and can't stop and get more or less hypnotized by it. Occasionally, people throw a fit, an anger fit.

After all, the Good Book says, "BE STILL and KNOW I AM GOD." The I AM Within you. We are all parts of that one fabulous flame that is the reality, that spiritual flame, sparks of that one flame. There isn't a person here or wandering the Earth that isn't immortal. How are they learning their lessons here? Or how much of the lessons are they learning? **Each one of you is the judge for yourself what you wish to change or not to change in your living. But the Super Bowl is to slide into that place where you just love everyone with that great compassion.** Even if they're an enemy of yours.

An attitude you might have is whoever they are, whatever they're doing, within them is that same immortal spark that is within you. If you want a better part than the one you're playing in this lifetime in future lifetimes, you better go to work at it, hadn't you? Straighten up and fly right a little bit.

When ships that go to sea get barnacles on the bottom, you don't

have to scrape them off. All you do is run the vessel into pure, clear water and the barnacles fall off. That pure consciousness within is located in the heart. That's where that pure part is. It's watching you. As much as it can get through to you it will. You're its special care for the incarnation, hoping that you will FALL AWAKE a little bit and feel that reality.

It isn't a matter of thinking it. I've known people who have read thousands of books and have no more feeling than that hunk of wood right there. It's the FEELING of love! Love is a subtle thing. Yet, it is the easiest thing in the world. When you see a beautiful little child, your heart goes right out to them.

Find that part of you that recognizes that Godliness everywhere, which is pure love. If you want to make it anthropomorphic, it represents some great teacher. **But you have to do it for you. No one else can do it for you.** If you've taken somebody else's word for things and haven't tried it out in your living, that don't count. It's got to be an experience of yourself where you actually FEEL it!

More of our emotions are on the surface of our bodies, normally, than within. Until we hit the big One, and then we feel it, it's just there.

When you see a situation that's difficult, and you're not even involved with it, you'll have enough feeling of empathy to send that love toward it, so that it will create that harmony. There is harmony in the universe! Not in our social structure, no. But if you go out at night and look up at the clear blue sky and see all the stars in their orbits continually for centuries, you know there is a law functioning. If you realize that winter, spring, summer, fall come along very regularly every year, you know there is something of an eternal harmony underneath it all. **All we have to do is tune ourselves into that greater harmony. We've already got a hotline to it within each and every one of us. If you can just be still, and feel it.**

It's much more pleasant to feel love than to feel hate. We can talk of love and associate it with just sex, that's still love. It's the attraction of love. But when you get to that place in your heart, it's being attracted to Godhood and you start feeling the universal part. Then whoever they are, you try to let them feel your love. You send them a feeling of love.

Even if you meet some people that you think you're so much smarter than that they don't even belong to your section, remember every single one of them has the same spark within them. Even those cows, and I love to eat beef, everyone of 'em has that same spark coming through in its evolution.

This isn't something that you have to go have someone tell you about. Because you've already got it. But you're not using it. You always meet someone who causes that FLASH to come, that FLASH from inside, the pure feeling of love! That's the most important thing. You can tune into this other part of yourself, this higher consciousness, this love for humanity. You have to love humanity as a whole because you know there is only One behind it all and I don't think it's a guy with a long white beard. It's a Force.

I like those movies that came out with, **"May the Force be with you!"** I hope the same thing, may the force be with all of you. Every time I say, "Ya Fatah!" I'm thinking and feeling that, because I'm kind of fumbly-bumbly yet. So if I can't just feel it by itself, I know if I say the words and put my mind on the trip, that it will surrender to the higher part within me and give out love. **LIVE LOVE!**

After all, I'm a pretty good recommendation even for the limited aspect that I represent: I'm eighty-four years old and I haven't got a lumbago or rheumatism. I must be doing something right, I can't be all wrong. It's working for me to that extent, and I think for as little as I understand it, that's a very broad extent.

I don't know if any of you sitting in here will pay any attention to anything I say, and that don't make any difference. Because the seeds are being planted within you, a stimulation to that part of you. At least, you met one old fogey once who told you what it was all about.

Sure, you get back into this level of down here on Earth and in these bodies, just the attraction of another person is what makes all our advertisements go. We never see any ugly women advertising anything. We never see any puny men like me on TV advertising anything. It's only the heroic figure who can cause a little irritation of that part of that part of our anatomy that's always pulling toward the opposite sex.

If you're gonna have love, make it big! If you're going to have physical love, make it so that you have a higher aspiration that you wanna FALL AWAKE! If both of you have got that feeling the male-female interest will be just as vital. Come on. You've got a chance. You come here to hear this old fossil who doesn't know a hell of a lot. But nevertheless, I'm trying to share with you what I've dug out of it. I want you to get the feel of it.

When we're quiet, just before we go to sleep or just after we wake up and feel the glory in ourselves, what a wonderful feeling. The founder of the Theosophical Society, H.P.B., said for you to realize, just like the first thing that happens to you when you wake up in the morning, I AM. You know you are because you're awake. That's all you can say, I AM. Other than that I AM, what you're wearing here are very limited tools compared to what you have within you that you could use. You each find it in your own way. Some little event will occur to you, you'll see something, grab it if it's there for a second and you feel that complete love flowing out. **Keep it alive, very alive!**

Sure, there are disciplines, practices too. Some of them are very fine. If they weren't good for the people at the level they are, they wouldn't be doing them. But each one of you are individuals at this level, so each one of you has to find the particular thing that will bring to you a broader concept of what it is all about. It can't be much broader than that it's all a Oneness.

This particular life is very important. You have to meet life day by day. There is no particular pattern that can be given to you that will explain each crisis you will meet as you go along. What would be better than the internal harmony of the oneness of God, the feeling of that love? If you live a certain way, you think, "Well, at the end of this it's just gonna all be over, and there's nothing else. There's just a blank and I'm done." That's not true.

When a person slips out of this body—because the only thing that dies is the thing you're wearing—the reality of you and your consciousness does not die. You find yourself on the astral plane with the same feelings that you had here. Just because you die doesn't give you the rights to a pair of wings or a ride on the lightning, huh? Come on. You got to FALL AWAKE here!

What I have learned and I'm trying to use, I want to pass that on, just as one person to another. I don't see any clairvoyant visions. I don't have some spirits come and visit me. I don't have someone play some special kind of music, so that I can go into a trance. Nothing like that. I'm just taking it from here, my heart and my own deep thinking and deep feeling. I've found out that LOVE works out best.

There isn't anybody as low as you might consider them to be. You go down on the other side of Market Street and look at some of those people who are hooked on the wine bottle and say, "Oh, too bad. He's got a fixation." Well, you never stop to think of whatever fixation *we've* got that's holding us in the particular position we're in and keeping us from getting somewhere. Think it over.

But you see where I want to get is not somewhere, I want to get NOWHERE! I want to get to the reality Itself where it all comes from. When you find the way of going with love, you always have the effervescence and that feeling that the great masters who came understood, feeling

that way toward other people and helping them to grow.

The Spiritual Teachings of Ramana Maharshi

I don't know how you are going to feel when I get through with this talk, but I'm going to let you have it!

Ramana Maharshi was born before the turn of the century. He passed away in the fifties. He brought something in the line of Vedanta philosophy. As you know, all philosophies, in essence, are of the very Oneness itself. It's simply that different peoples have had different ways to explain the life of the spirit.

Ramana Maharshi brought something so very revolutionary. He did not have a personal teacher. There were just experiences that he went through as a very young man. Once, in his room, he said, "Look, Ramana, you're dead." He really felt as if he were not there. But then he said that he wasn't dead. It was just his body that was dead. He couldn't move any of it. He couldn't look in any direction other than the way he was looking.

That experience brought through to him the fact that the consciousness phase, the real I, never dies. It never dies. It was never born. It is immortal. **It is the essence of reality.** Bodies come and bodies go, whether you believe in reincarnation or not is up to you. But in believing in reincarnation, understand that the real you is never born and never dies. In other words, I could say, "Would the real you please stand up," and there it would be, if you were clairvoyant enough to see it.

That essence within you is already perfect. The difficulties are that which you have taken on in going through incarnation in order to learn about life and come to the realization of what you are. So, in one way, there is no reincarnation and, in another way, there very definitely is such a thing. The spiritual essence is indestructible, immortal, invisible yet felt at every moment.

So, in the meantime, Ramana went to live in Tiruvanamali. The little children there thought he was simply pretending to be a holy man and they threw rocks at him. So he had to hide himself down in a deep place inside the temple there. He was trying to come to his own understanding. In other words, he took it all from within himself. Therefore, it had to be something that he brought with him into that particular incarnation.

In answer to the questions put to him, Ramana dictated a very small pamphlet entitled "Who Am I?" In answering questions, he would tell the person to ask simply, "Who am I?" Now, at first, that might sound like a silly question. But it is not. When you wake up in the morning, what is the first thing you are conscious of? It's you, YOU. You are conscious of that I inside. You know it's not somebody down the block. It is not somebody else, it's you! So Ramana simply said if you keep asking yourself, "Who am I?" and trace back and eliminate everything else, you finally come to the reality of what YOU are. Then you start acting in spontaneity with true spiritual direction.

In the same way you might say, "I'm doing the will of the Father," using Christian terminology. But you do not have to look all over for the Father. I can assure you the Father is not an old man sitting up in the clouds with a long white beard. If you want to picture it that way, that's up to you.

Now there are billions of people in incarnation at this time because we are coming to the end of an epoch. All the beings that deserve a chance with this particular stream of evolution are in incarnation now. It is supposed to all be straightened out by the end of this century. I don't know what that augurs for the future.

But I hope that when I get through talking to you that you will understand at least part of what I am trying to tell you. I am not going to tell it to you in very literate language. I am just someone who has studied these teachings and has been working at it since 1924, trying to dig out the nitty-gritty so I can share it with other people.

When something came along, I tried it. I decided to keep at it. I wanted to keep digging to find out more. As long as something held my interest and I felt I was getting something out of it, I would go for it. But when it is done, don't say, "Well, this is all there is, I got to stay here." Let your consciousness expand. You might say, "Well, that's all right, you have had some wonderful experiences, but I am just an ordinary person." Who isn't an ordinary person? **All human beings have the same spark in their hearts.**

Now you are in the waking state. When you go to sleep, at first you dream then you go into deep sleep. After that, you start it all over again. In Sanskrit, that part in which you are awake is called *jagrat*. That part in which you dream is called *svapna*. The deep sleep stage is called *sushupti*. Because when you are in that clear state, your senses are not with you. You are in your spiritual body.

You are at one with the reality all the time, although you don't know it. You are like a ship. You have got a lot of barnacles on your hull. You need to be rolled out of the ocean into fresh water, in order to get those barnacles off and realize you are THAT now! The ship is your consciousness. The barnacles are the concepts that you have built up over lifetimes, and the fresh water is the Clear Light which you are in essence.

Realization, non-realization, these are attitudes and viewpoints you hold. When you are really awake, this is as much a dreamland as any dream is.

When you wake up in the morning, you say, "Boy, I feel better today. I feel better than I did yesterday. I had a good sleep." How do you know you had a good sleep? How do you know? You know because in the waking, dreaming, deep sleep states, there is something called *turiya*, an awareness of it all. This *turiya*, this awareness, the spiritual part of you never sleeps. It never sleeps. It is an awareness you come to within yourself. That part of you has to be carried from this waking state through the dream state into the deep sleep state.

When you have carried it through and still have it in this consciousness in the world, then you are getting beyond the wheel that is holding you kidnapped. Otherwise, you are going around and around in the events that happen in your body. Sure, you are learning by it. But your home is with you all the time. You can be in that spiritual center. It is just a question of whether or not you can be still. Can you be still? Can you be very still? Can you be so still that none of your thoughts are bugging you? Can you be in that place all the time? The Buddhists call it "Clear Light."

Ramana says ask yourself, "Who am I?" Not the limited I that says "I" but that which is behind it and vivifies it and gives it life. That is in you now. You don't have to go to India, Timbuktu, or the moon to contact the reality. It is within each one of you and you have to find it for yourself! The bhakti way is to go to the heart and use pure love. **But what I'm talking about tonight is pure jnani, pure mind. If you can take it, you can take it! If you can't, you can't.** [19]

Figure out how you want to get there. Do you want to use your feelings to make yourself pure enough that you love anything and everything, pure enough that there isn't anything you do not love? Can you love anything and everything because you realize it is all a Oneness and it is part of you and you are part of it? Then when you look at someone, you are looking at yourself out of their eyes. Will you go that far? Can you take a person you despise and say, "I love you," and really mean it? If you can, you are pure *bhakti*. But the *bhakti* and the *jnani*, the feeling and the knowing, have to come together in the one understanding and finding of this reality.

If you think I am making this up out of my own head, I'm not. It is based on *The Spiritual Teachings of Ramana Maharshi*. I am trying to drive it deep into your heads and hearts. I want to help you dig into it. I spent years trying to find out about these things. The reality is alive within each one of you now. It's just that you cannot believe it. Another thing Ramana says stands in the way, is that we say, "Oh well, others can do that. But I am not ready for it. I don't know, I'm too ignorant."

Ignorance, the shadow, is the only obstacle that stands in the way of everyone in this room being fully realized right at this very moment. Now, the first awareness might come to you in a moment when you are terribly frightened. Maybe you are confronted by someone with a gun, or you are driving your car and find yourself in a bind, and you don't know how you are going to get out. Did you ever notice how clear everything becomes? You see all the details, just like that, because you have stopped this peripheral thinking and you have referred to the higher mind and consciousness, to that super-subtle state known as Buddhi. Now, that is right next door to Atma. If you have touched the Buddhi or universal aspect, you are right next to touching Atma.

Now, a friend of mine, S. S. Cohen wrote something which I would like to read you:

> Now what you should do is to learn what the Self is, and then di-rectly seek it. Do not digress in irrelevant matters, in bodies, koshas, involution and evolution, birth and death; in supersensuous sights and sounds, etc. for all these are glamorous irrelevancies which trap and seduce you away from the reality of yourself and retain you in the delusion of the senses from which you are now attempting to escape. What is of importance is not what you perceive, think or do, but WHAT YOU ARE. Sense-perceptions, conception, sensa-tions, actions are mere pictures in the consciousness that perceives them. They rise from it, like dreams from the dreamer, distract its attention for awhile and disappear in it. They change incessantly, have a beginning and an end, but he, the thinker and knower, be-ing pure intelligence, remains ever. The knower is indestructible. The light of knowledge comes only from him, the subject, never the object, the body. What we therefore call our Self is not the body, which is born, grows and dies, which is made of innumerable non-homogeneous parts which do not think, do not seek, do not

perceive and do not understand. We are the intelligent indivisible unit "I"—life itself—which pervades and uses the body, which sees but cannot be seen, hears but cannot be heard, smells but cannot be smelt, knows but cannot be known: for always it is a subject, never an object. And because we cannot see, hear or smell our "I," we mistake it for the body which can be seen, heard and smelt. Thus the self-instinct, the "I" sense, getting mixed up with the sense-perceptions, loses itself in the world of sense-precepts, from which none can save it but the supreme guide, the divine guru.

Reflections on Talks with Sri Ramana Maharshi, p. viii.

Now this supreme guide, this divine guru is within each one of us—that is a heavy statement I just read, isn't it? In other words, most of us sitting here, I know I figured it this way for years, think that body you are carrying around is you. But it is just something we are using. It is not you. And that which I'm using is not me. There is another part within there that is immortal which you can get to. And that is what I want to try to help you get to. But only you can do it for you!

I don't care if you sit and concentrate on your navel for all eternity, it is not going to give it to you. You've got to feel it and be it! It is in the being, not in the thinking.

With pure love, you are at one with it. As far as most outer knowledge goes, there comes a time when you sweep it all in the dustpan and throw it in the garbage can. Because you will be functioning from that very Oneness, and then you will know with that Oneness, what you are to do. That's a wonderful gift if you can grab it. If you can't, that's all right too. Sooner or later, you have to come to it. At least, you have heard about it. So, sooner or later, when one of the things that you have put up as a symbol of perfection goes all to pieces, you will realize that you're still here, and it is within you and every one of us.

Whatever way you want to move toward it, that is wholly up to you. When you stop to think of it, I am trying to say in words what is *The Secret of The Ages*. I'm trying to convey in words what cannot be conveyed in words. Yet maybe you will get a feel for it on the overtone.

All right, how do you come in contact with this in ordinary time, how do we come into this Real I? When you are working at something, just routine work, you just keep on doing it. Whether or not people are there doesn't really matter. You are just floating. You are just going along with the flow of it, like a mighty river.

We are separate in as much as we are all original, but we are still at one with the light, life, and love. You see, it is not a concept. You could say I have this concept and I am going to be this. **IT IS NOT IN CONCEPTS!** It is in the spontaneous something that you *are*. You might say, "I'm going to figure this out logically, I'll do it in this way, this way and this way." Then you will look at it and say, "It won't work." Then all of a sudden something inside of you happens and you just do it.

Find that part that doesn't count in the western world. This society is all focused on gain, loss and duality. You're looking for the Oneness, and that Oneness is what each of us has and is as well as being so collectively.

People would come and ask Ramana questions like:

There are times when person and things take a vague, almost transparent form, as in a dream. One ceases to observe them as outside, but is passively conscious of their existence, while not actively conscious of any kind of selfhood. There is a deep quietness in the mind. Is it at such times that one is ready to dive into the Self? Or is this condition unhealthy, the result of self-hypnotism? Should it be encouraged as yielding temporary peace?

And Ramana would answer:

There is consciousness along with quietness in the mind; this is exactly the state to be aimed at. The fact that the question has been framed on this point, without realizing that it is the Self, shows the state is not steady but casual. The word "diving" is appropriate when there are outgoing tendencies, and when, therefore, the mind has to be directed and turned within, there is a dip below the surface of externalities. But when quietness prevails without obstructing the consciousness, where is the need to dive? If that state has not been realized as the Self, the effort to do so may be called "diving." In this sense, the state may be said to be suitable for realization or diving. Thus, the last two questions you have put do not arise.

Spiritual Teachings of Ramana Maharshi, pp. 61-62.

In other words, suppose you get through with your day's work, you are sitting in front of the television. You are not particularly interested in the show. You are just sitting there. You are not awake, and yet, you are not asleep. But you are perfectly clear and it feels great. Right in that stage of your consciousness is where it is.

Anytime you can just cool it and be still, it is there. The point is to stop the thing from running the way it wants to and let it run the way the real part of you wants it to run. The whole point is just that. This isn't out of some college somewhere. This isn't a thousand miles away on a high mountain. It is inside of each one of us.

Every great religion has pointed out the same truth. But just to read it isn't going to do it. That would simply be putting another tape in your head. And tapes are like newspapers, after awhile they pile up so high that there is no place for you to be. Where's the real you? Be sure that you consult the real you now and then. It is just making the mind be still so that the heart, the Thatness can speak to you. Because THAT is God, the higher mind, the higher reality. That is where it is in you. You can forget about it, if you have to. I don't care what you try. Sooner or later, when everything on the outside goes against you, you'll say there must be something somewhere. And if you turn to some anthropomorphic being, that is your way of doing it. But the other way is to simply say, "Thine not mine be done."

A person said to me, "Well, look what's happening to me!" I said, "It doesn't say you're going to get what you want. It says you'll get what you need." Karmic things come down, so what? You've got to bleed it out of your sub-conscious before you are wide enough awake to look at the reality and realize it is as close as your jugular vein. It isn't just somebody handing you a snow-job. You have to dig it out of yourself. It is there. There is no place it isn't. There is nothing that is not of the very Oneness itself. Realize that! Try it.

If you are angry at someone, look at the person and say, "That's another part of me, all right, I'll be kind to him." There is a big job. Can you just be kind to everybody? If you can, you are going in the right direction. This is for real. I don't know where it is going to take me. But it has let me get by for eighty years, anyhow.

Now, I am not saying this is the way you have got to do it. You are going to do what you want. Nobody gets anybody else to do anything. The person makes up his/her own mind and then he/she goes ahead and does it. You can make suggestions. But nobody can look inside your head and into your heart and think your thoughts or have your feelings. You do it individually.

Carl Gustav Jung, the psychologist, wrote his introduction to *The Spiritual Teachings of Ramana Maharshi*. Usually, what he has said concerning the Eastern methods is, "Well, that's all right for the East. But it's no good for the West. They cannot do that over here. They do not understand it."

But in this introduction, he says something quite different:

Sri Ramana is a true son of the Indian earth. He is genuine and, in addition to that, something quite phenomenal. In India, he is the whitest spot in a white space. What we find in the life and teachings of Sri Ramana Maharshi is the purest of India; with its breadth of world-liberated and liberating humanity, it is a chant of millenniums. This melody is built on a single, great motif, which in a thousand colorful reflexes, rejuvenates itself within the Indian spirit, and the latest incarnation of which is Sri Ramana Maharshi himself. The identification of the Self with God will strike the European as shocking. It is a specifically oriental realization, as expressed in Sri Ramana's utterances. Psychology cannot contribute anything further to it, except the remark that it lies far beyond its scope to propose such a thing.

Spiritual Teachings of Ramana Maharshi, pp. vii-x.

So much for the psychologists that are trying to tell you how to live a real mystical life. Here is one of the biggest men in the business saying that what Ramana says is beyond it.

Now I will just skip ahead to the finish:

The provision with all "necessities" is, without doubt, a source of happiness which is not to be underestimated. But above and beyond it, the inner man raises his claim, which cannot be satisfied by any external goods: and the less this voice is heard in the hunt for "wonderful things" of this world, the more the inner man becomes a source of inexplicable bad luck and ununderstandable unhappiness in the midst of conditions of life from which one would expect something quite different. The externalization leads to an incurable suffering, because nobody can understand how one could suffer because of one's own nature. Nobody is surprised at his own insatiability, but looks upon it as his birthright; he does not realize that the one-sidedness of the diet of his soul ultimately leads to the most serious disturbances of balance. It is this which forms the illness of the westerner, and he does not rest until he has infected the whole world with his greedy restlessness. The wisdom and mysticism of the East have, therefore, a great deal to tell us, provided they speak their own inimitable speech. They should remind us of what we possess in our own culture of similar things and have long since forgotten, and direct our attention to that which we put aside as unimportant, namely the destiny of our inner man. The life and teachings of Sri Ramana are not only important for the Indian but also for the westerner. Not only do they form a record of great human interest, but also a warning message to a humanity which threatens to lose itself in the chaos of its unconsciousness and lack of self-control.

That was written by one of the best psychological minds the world has produced. I feel that a hundred years from now in regard to the teachings of Ramana Maharshi, everybody will say, "Well, of course, everybody knows that." But right now, it's "What is this? This is crazy."

The teaching is to make the mind, the lower mind, quiet and find your own way to the higher mind, the heart, whether you do it by meditation or by *bhakti*. Those are the two ways you can go. This is not something far in the distance. Anything I have said tonight is about use. This is something you can do. Americans love that. It is a do-it-yourself kit. You have got to have an intimate experience of the ultimate.

I would like you to do a little meditation with me, just try being still. I think you will find that the effect of my having your attention for so long has created something that will make it possible for you to feel a little bit of it for yourself. Be still, be very still.

The Sutra of Hui-Neng

Now I want to tell you a little of the background of how I got interested in Hui-Neng. To begin with, I heard about the Sutra of Wei-Lang, that was quite a number of years ago, before they decided the proper way to spell it was Hui-Neng.

I got this sutra and I took it to my apartment. I read it. Then I read it again. Then I read it late that night. Then I took it out and threw it in the garbage chute. I said, "There isn't anything else I need to know. It's all right there." That was it. I was very impetuous in those days. Later, I said to myself, "What did that guy say in such and such a verse in such a chapter?" But it was so complete that it triggered something.

Now let me tell you a little something about Hui-Neng. Hui-Neng could neither read nor write. He was illiterate. But he became the Sixth Patriarch in that particular line of these teachings. Bodhidharma was the first guy to break out of the routine. They had quite a conglomeration of different religions and different ways of how to approach Buddhism. Bodhidharma decided "this is a lot of hooey." He figured, "If it's anywhere, it's not in the books, not in the teachings of what somebody who didn't know has put down. It's got to be something that is me and I'm it!"

The experience is what counts. That's why in our particular group I always encourage rebels because I don't want people that are going to lay down and let somebody walk on them like a rug. People have to figure it out for themselves. That's the reason the Hui-Neng Sutra has such a pull for me.

The front end of the sutra gives you a little idea about where this fellow Hui-Neng came from: he is living in the city, taking care of his aged mother. His father has been banished from that part of the country for picking the wrong political party. Whether or not they killed the old man isn't said. Hui-Neng was a young fellow. He didn't have any particular trade or academic background. He couldn't read or write. So, other than chopping bamboo now and then, he would go around in the alleys and pick up all the sticks of wood, tie them together in packages and sell them for firewood. It was a rather rough way of living.

One day, Hui-Neng is out selling wood, and he hears someone repeat part of the Diamond Sutra. When he heard one verse, he knew right away what it meant. So he asked this fellow, reciting the sutra, "Where do you come from?" And the guy answered, "I come from the Fifth Patriarch, and anyone can go there to study with him if they wish."

Hui-Neng wanted to go, because he knew he had dug what it was all about. Somebody gave him ten silver teals, which was enough for him to provide for the care of his mother for the rest of her life. So he took off on foot to get to the Fifth Patriarch's monastery.

Naturally, the Fifth Patriarch questioned any new members coming into the monastery, and he said, "Well, what do you want?" Hui-Neng says, "All I want is to be a Buddha, that's all." So this guy looks at him and says, "You come from the South and you think you can become a Buddha?"

Hui-Neng says, "Whether you come from the South or the North, whether it's you or me, anyone has the Bodhi seed within them. Anyone can become a Buddha." The Fifth Patriarch said, "This guy talks too much, put him out in the barn and let him grind rice." So Hui-Neng went and ground rice.

When the Fifth Patriarch was getting pretty old, he decided there should be someone in the group who had caught the spark of the reality. If someone had caught the spark of the reality, he would give that one his robe and bowl. This would represent the passing on of authority, so that one would be the Sixth Patriarch. There were about a thousand guys attending the monastery. They all decided it wasn't going to do any good for any of them to write a sutra because they had all been studying with Shen Hsiu. He was their teacher. They all figured, "We'll leave it up to him because he's the one that obviously should get the robe and be the next patriarch."

Shen Hsui realized what they were thinking about him, so he went to his room to write a poem. But how are you going to present this to the old man without him thinking that you're so egotistical you want to get his robe? You want to be the head man, but ambition is frowned on in the Buddhist community, from the standpoint of their hierarchy anyway. You know what I mean, "Ambitious? Oh no, I wouldn't wanna be . . . ." So he figured out that the head man would be down in the corridor because they were going to put some paintings up. These were to tell the lives of the great ones and so forth. Shen Hsui copped himself a sneak down to the corridor and wrote on the wall.

What he wrote on the wall about having the dharma and knowing it read:

Our body is the bodhi tree,
And our mind the mirror bright.
Carefully we wipe them hour by hour,
And let no dust alight.

The Patriarch comes along and he's got this artist with him and he says, "There's no use you putting any paintings on the wall, this is great. Have some candles lit and some incense sent down." Then he left the hall and he called the fellow to see him. He said, "You put that on the wall. People who follow it will be closer to an understanding, but it shows you haven't got the Enlightenment yet." He said, "You recite the poem as much as you want. It'll be good for you." "Our mind is the mirror bright . . . .." All right. "We wipe them hour by hour and let no dust alight . . . .." All right, okay. So Hui-Neng hears this sutra recited. Hui-Neng says, "What's that?" The other guy says, "You really are ignorant. That's in the hall and you haven't seen it. I'll take you there and show you." So he took him to the place and Hui-Neng looked at it.

> The boy took me there and I asked him to read it to me, as I am illiterate. A petty officer of the Chiang Chou district named Chang Tih Yung, who happened to be there, read it out to me. When he had finished reading, I told him that I also had composed a stanza, and asked him to write it for me. "Extraordinary, indeed," he exclaimed, "that you also can compose a stanza." "Don't despise a beginner," said I, "if you are a seeker of supreme enlightenment. You should know that the lowest class may have the sharpest wit, while the highest may be in want of intelligence. If you slight others, you commit a very great sin." "Dictate your stanza," said he. "I will take it down for you. But do not forget to deliver me, should you succeed in getting dharma!"
>
> *The Sutra of Hui-Neng*, p. 15.

I imagine that set the officer back on his heels plenty. So this is what Hui-Neng had the man write for him:

There is no bodhi tree,
Nor stand of a mirror bright.
Since all is void,
Where can the dust alight?

Okay. Now right away, at the very beginning in this first chapter of the book, it's within that verse! If you could dig what's there, you'd have it. But the chances are it's more or less goobley-gook to you. Now I can't go through this whole book for you, but I can give you some of the salient points. All through the book, Hui-Neng is answering questions from left field, right field, no field at all and coming up with answers that seem to bring enlightenment to the people who came to see him. So I think this is a very valuable book. It's so valuable that I won't throw it away again.

The bodhi tree, that part of you, doesn't grow, doesn't diminish. It can't be cut down. It's already perfect. It's like a ship that comes in from the sea, the bottom of the ship is covered with barnacles. They don't go out there with a chisel and chisel them off. You know what they do? They run it into clear water and the barnacles just fall off. So if you can find the clear light within you, the clear understanding, if you can say "Look, I'm not a worm crawling on the ground. In that essence of my being, I am that reality now! It isn't something I'm going to earn over a certain number of years, it's already here and the only thing that's standing in the way of me realizing it is me." **Sounds wild, doesn't it? It is wild, he was wild.**

They would say to Hui-Neng, "I know a man in a very terrible condition," and he'd say, "I know a man in a very wonderful condition." In other words, any question that was put to him, he'd answer it with antonyms. By telling them just the opposite they'd drop into the common sense between and realize that any positive and negative at any phase whatsoever are just opposite poles of the same energy.

So you say, "Well, suppose I have a limitation in my vehicle," or somebody pushes me on my butt and I break my hip. Why should that happen to me, I didn't do anything? I didn't feel that way at all. When I got home, I said to Guin, "I think I got my comeuppance for some other times I owed." At least, I'm done with it now, I don't need to bother. But for me to feel anger at the guy or wanna kill him or beat him up, that wouldn't have been so effective. It was another test. Life is full of tests to help us get straightened out and clear. Whether we like it or not. If we won't clear it up with simple tests, they get tougher — and tougher. So you got to come out of it and see where you're at; you gotta realize that everyone living on this planet, all animate beings, and the life itself on this planet are One!

When you look into somebody else's eyes, you're looking at yourself whether you like it or not. It may be in a rather odd shape, but that's neither here nor there. You gotta find out for yourself. Then you say, "Oh well, I know but after all, I have to go through all these initiations, I gotta study these libraries of books." NO! You don't have to do that to drop inside of yourself and just look at it. See it. See it with a single eye. As it says in the Good Book, **"If your eye be single, your being will be filled with light."**

The feeling of just deep joy, that's one of the first things that the fellow who signs up to be a bodhisattva experiences, **great joy**. Because you realize it's all ONE! You realize that everything we're into here is a movie, and yet, it's for real at the particular time at this level. But from that awareness observe it. Nothing to sweat about. It's already done. As Guin always says to me when I start emoting about something, "Look, your rice was cooked from the beginning." That's another way the Chinese had of saying the same thing, because you're already perfect in that part of you.

There's something good in everything. But where are you and what do you want? How much do you sit down and do a little retrospecting without condemning yourself? Look at everything you think you did wrong. "Well, by the way that person looked at me I could see that they didn't like me and I don't want to . . . ." FORGET IT! **You gotta live! You've go to radiate love to people. This book is so strictly American. America is great for Do-It-Yourself.** The Hui-Neng Sutra is something that you can do for you. And so you say, "Well, how will I know if I reach the Futzacutsa?" Well, I tell you, you'll know because of the sureness of feeling within yourself, a certain knowing. Look, it's beyond what we call knowledge. Spell knowledge for me—K N O W L E D G E. I'm not very good at spelling, I'm kind of illiterate myself, but it says *NO-LEDGE*! When you push off of the *NO-LEDGE* into the realization and the feel of it, is when you get it! You study all these things. Right? They tell you the direction but if the power hasn't started to happen within you and you don't feel it, you ain't got it. If the feeling is just for something that you gotta have and possess for yourself, **that's not it**. That's sentimentality. But if the feeling is for everyone and a great joy and you know it's there, **that's it**. Mindlessness, thoughtlessness. **But be very mindful.**

Hui-Neng says that those who sit up against a wall and think only of a wall, all they're doing is putting a concept in their heads that a wall is it. That ain't it. The only thing that particular discipline or exercise does is to quiet down the lower mind so that maybe you can come into just a touch of where the bodhi heart is at. Bodhi heart, okay—in his book on the Mahayana, someone asked and they have put down what they consider the bodhi heart, explaining it: "Bodhi heart is the inner perception of absolute wisdom and all-embracing love that pours forth as compassion for all living beings. It is the seed of truth in the spiritual heart of mankind, the fruition of which is Buddhahood." That little paragraph is loaded. Dig that, dig that. Possessive love is just the early stages of finding out about it, you're just growing a little. Then after a bit, you find out that there is just so much love flowing out from you that you love everybody. You may not like them, but you sure do love them.

Take this Hui-Neng Sutra and read it until you think you know what's in there, then put the book on the shelf and look at it six months later. You'll wonder where the hell all the stuff came from that you didn't see the first time you read it. I laid upstairs today and my wife put up with me. There is so much in this book that I want to give people but I can't give it to them because you can't put it into words. It's in the subtle part of your being. It's there that each of you have to experience something. If somebody's saying, "Just be this, just do that and it'll be just this way," it won't work. It's a change of consciousness within you. You gotta go ahead and read about it and have somebody push you off of that *NO-LEDGE* (Knowledge) until you throw yourself on the very Oneness of the reality and start to experience it. And then, that's beautiful. They may look at you and say you're a little nuts after that, but to the extent that I can do it, I have a hell of a good time doing it.

It's just that place where you can look at everything that needs your help, you help it along. It don't mean you stop thinking, it don't mean that you stop having opinions. But underneath it all, through it all, is that love of the reality, and you know that everybody is a part of it. They're just trying to grow up to a place where they can FALL AWAKE individually and become aware of it. In the awareness is all. The only difference between an ignorant man and a Buddha is that the Buddha knows he's a Buddha and the ignorant man thinks he isn't. Of course, you can realize that this sort of teaching being promulgated in the East, where they had them do so many thousand prostrations, didn't do much good for the reputation of the particular outfit.

Ch'an. Ch'an is suppose to mean dhyana, but the very thing that he was pushing is what I'm trying to push and that's prajna, wisdom itself in activity within us. That we feel that and come alive to it, that's what we want! This doesn't mean for you to become a soft touch and when you go down the street every bum that braces you for a buck, you give him two. It isn't charity. He spoke to this one emperor who said, "I bought monasteries, I did this, I did that. What merit have I accumulated?" Hui-Neng said, "None." What I would say in our vernacular is all the guy was doing was shining the apple to make it easier on himself when he popped out of incarnation. He was worried about the way in which he had accumulated the money.

Forgiveness is automatic to anybody and for everybody, okay? All great religions teach this truth. Automatic! Christ said it is automatic. If you realize that we're all one being, who is there to forgive but ourselves? Regardless of what the hell comes down ! Huh? Okay? All right? We're all part of them and they're a part of us. It's a Oneness. Maybe you think it's a little heavy, it is heavy! Because believe me, that's the way I feel about it. Oh, we've got books back there that'll sell you astral real estate from here to kingdom come and back. You can have visions of floating on the head of a pin or being five buddhas going backward and moving up Mt. Tamalpais if you want. It isn't in the imagination, it's coming to that realness, and feeling that love for everybody. I think that's where the bodhi tree is, I know that's where the bodhi heart is!

Now if you think I'm biased in the direction of Buddhism, I'm not. I don't have any biases. All religions contain the same thing. It's a matter of you getting something that will get it through to you. And of course, to begin with, you're all nuts for being here. Anybody with any common sense knows that this is not based on any facts, it's not "scientific." I can't show you the bodhi heart, but dammit I can make you feel it, that's for sure. That's what I want you to do, feel it! It's not a matter of something that you can have on Sundays as many church-goers have looked at it. It's gotta be something that you have alive in you and you live from that part of you within outward. This gives you the chance to graduate from everything that's tying you up in your personal life.

As a matter of fact many times you'll find yourself acting upon that part of yourself intuitively, without any mental process whatsoever. Logic and reasoning is excellent for living in the world, but for finding out what you are in the depth of you, you have to turn within. And when you find it within, you find it's without also. You find that you individually have a guide book that's your own particular possession, because of the experience that you've been through not only in this incarnation but in many other incarnations. So you live it from there. You see there are a lot of people nowadays that are in mental institutions and if they had gotten a hold of things in the nature of what you people are getting, they'd have been all right. Regardless of how limited this particular tool, at least it's coming to you, at least you got together. The general run of the public would say you could be sitting in front of the boob tube and getting your eyes as big as musk melons instead of going to hear that old idiot talk. But you see what hurts me is that I can't say it, it can't be said. It can't be written. Weird, isn't it?

It's a dream in one way. We're caught in the dream. You all have dreams. Sometimes you have a nightmare and you're hoping to God you wake up because it looks so horrible. That's a dream too. Believe me, when you get hurt in a dream, you feel hurt. You could dream you were starving to death and even though you had a full meal before you went to sleep, you'd probably starve to death if you didn't wake up in time. Now we're into dreaming, deep sleep and the reality that is behind, through and over it all—the Oneness, the Thatness, the Be-Ness, Christ, Krishna . . . .I don't care what name you put on it! One could go on interminably because the various teachers have come to the various levels of humanity, the various nationalities, to get to them as clearly as possibly they could some understanding of the reality of who they were and they weren't, so that they could JUST BE! [20]

Sufis Are Seed

Flowers come up out of the ground and shed their beauty and fragrance. They purify the air and make it possible for us to breathe. If all the greenery was gone, we wouldn't be able to breathe or have any sustenance. They take all the poisons that are in the air and through distilling them with their very being they bring light and love.

That's what the Sufis have to do. The flowers don't say anything. They don't have any conversation with you. They're just there. But they're doing their job all the time. And from their place in the hierarchy of the planet, they're bringing love, purification, and light.

Each of you can be like one of the roses. And you are, in a sense, whether you know it or not. Come on! Either you're putting it back poison for poison, or you're purifying it with the love of Allah in your hearts! You don't need to say anything to people. Just go by. You're always turning to the left. Why are you doing that? You're turning around to that heart within you, the Mosque of Allah, within your living bodies at all times. *Feel it.* Let the fragrance flow through.

This Mevlevi Order was founded by Rumi whirling as he followed the beat of the goldsmith and was lifted into ECSTASY! When you're dancing it isn't just a matter of you moving around physically, the very heavenly hosts themselves are bringing you love and light to help you understand. This is not your permanent home. We're all visitors here from there. And I mean it seriously, I'm not a dope. Neither are you for being here. Though a lot of the populace might think you are, seeing you go around in circles.

Go deep within in your prayers and practices and find that reality, and it will lift you right out of yourselves. The Sufis are not the regular run of things that happen. The Sufis were placed here as seed, even as the flowers are placed here to bring joy and beauty.

She Is the Creator

Now some statements have been made about the ladies, the feminine aspect, that I don't agree with. So a dear friend of mine made a point of it to look up this passage in the *Mathnawi*, the main work of Rumi, and I would like to say this, in the NAME OF ALLAH WHO IS MERCY AND COMPASSION . . . .

> There's a tradition that Muhammed said,
> "A wise man will listen and be led by
> a woman, while ignorant men won't."
>
> Someone too fiercely connected to animal needs
> lacks kindness and the gentle affection that
> keeps men human. Anger and urgent desire
>
> are animal qualities, while a loving
> tenderness toward women shows someone
> no longer caged in with his wantings.
>
> The core of the feminine comes directly as
> a ray of the sun. She's not the earthy figure
> you hear about in lovesongs. There's more to her
>
> mystery than that. You might say she's not
> from the manifested world at all,
> but the *creator* of it. [21]

None of us are just creatures or animals. We're immortal beings learning about life in the body. When this was written, it was written for a purpose. The man was living half-way across the world in another country with the situation being what it was at that time, but remember, Allah KNOWS because it is all part of His Consciousness!

Women in this country are going to come into their own. And in other writings given in the sacred teachings it is said that in this coming century, the women will be the ones. Of course, men are immortal but women are a bit more than that. Women give life to men! Both emotionally and physically. It's a new age, a new world we're living in. The potentiality for the feminine side is tremendous. You men have the job of nurturing that.

In its pure state. And you can do it.

And only one leader of all the Sufis in those other countries, Suleyman Dede, had the courage to come to America and say that women should be included in the turning, the Sema, and that was a revolutionary thing for him to do. Remember, he passed his power on to my dear friend, Jelaluddin Loras. He is Pir of the Mevlevis from now on.

Maybe I'm sticking my neck way out, if I am may Allah strike me dead, but I wanted to get that message through to you . . . .Sam Lewis said it for the S.I.R.S. a long time ago. But this is from the teachings of Rumi, and it is my honor to bring it to you. **I presume that from one standpoint the boys might consider I'm rather foolish, but I'm not. I'm just showing them how much greater they are, because their brothers who are sisters are the ones who will be carrying the banner in the next century.**

Guin and Malika

Sufism

Well, you'll notice that in the title I just called it "Sufism." It didn't say what particular kind. I'm acquainted with a number of different kinds. I've met people associated with the Nimutallahi, Halveti, Mevlevi, Chisti . . . .

Now in regard to the Nimutallahi, I know Dr. Nurbaksh, one of their head guys. He wrote on something called *IRADAH*, in some other group this would be called "enlightenment" or "coming to enlightenment." He also said that those who are found acceptable as students should take the word of their teacher for everything until they had reached a further grade. This same rule holds good in all sufi orders, but this is America, and in America things are a bit different. We believe in a do-it-yourself kit. Therefore, this doesn't apply as fully here as it does in the Middle East where Sufism primarily came from.

But the same teachings came from other sources not called Sufism, called just *mysticism* if you will, and we have it in all of the great religions. My subject tonight is Sufism, so we're going to stick to Sufism. Dr. Nurbaksh wrote of *iradah* and that's from *heart to heart*. Getting it that way, and not getting it in words or, as it is listed in some of the teachings, as nafs. The lower mind and the intellect can't give it to you! It's purely a *bhakti* approach. The word *bhakti* means devotion, aspiration and pure love.

I presume a number of you here believe for sure that you know what love means. Most of you may be laboring under the false assumption that love is something of reciprocity among individuals. Well, it is in one way, but in its purest state LOVE means GIVING, not taking. GIVING, SHARING! The best way we use love in association with people is a very simple word—it's just being kind. Whatever the situation you find yourself in of irritation and troublesomeness with other individuals, use kindness in your approach.

I want to start a fire in all your hearts. I want you to feel love in its pure sense. Realize that when you come into the One in understanding as you find it, you'll find yourself so filled with love that it just has to radiate out. I'm talking on Sufism because it is a belief in the religion of the HEART. The big secret is within the spiritual heart, that spiritual heart within you is in the same space as your physical heart. That's the heart they're talking about . . . . **When you become so that you are consciously, intelligently and with love IN the DEPTH of your BEING, when you realize you are one and there is only ONE, it'll make all the difference in how you live. When you realize that the bodies you are wearing at this time are but the projection of part of your higher self for given experiences in this lifetime. A projection from within that depth of you that you can't get to at the moment. Most of you, I suppose. But you all will be able to.** This body is what you projected for certain experiences, to learn certain lessons you wanted to know at this level.

All of us are spiritual beings. We are all of the ONE in our physical expression. We can't express without the air we breathe. The organs within our bodies function without our knowledge of how they are to function. But in this age, in the latter part of the development of the mind, we're learning about these things from a mental standpoint. **According to some findings that the mystics of the past have written down, we are coming into an age when the intuitive factor within each one of us will start to awaken. Some ahead of others. They will know that there is that place beyond lower consciousness, the higher intelligence which is not of the lower mind. The lower mind is only using a fragment of that higher intelligence that resides within us.** But we have IT all the time in our lower minds. This particular vehicle that we are wearing, it is projected by the higher mind, and it has senses and these senses are what we are learning with. But what animates the sense is that intelligence, pure love, light and life. Light, love, and life are just three ways of saying the ONE.

When we become at one with that consciously, and work with it and listen to what comes from within our hearts, our higher self, then we can start to do the work of the One. Each of us has a certain niche in life to fill that we must find from within ourselves. All of the great Sufi masters only had their disciples with them usually long enough for THAT to awaken within each one of them. That was the particular thing that they were working on, to awaken that part. So they said there was a TRANSMISSION that was for the purpose of AWAKENING. When I say "awaken," a better word would be *aware*, to be AWARE of THAT at all times.

There were many great religions in the past that taught that this part of the world—the material plane—didn't mean anything at that particular level, the higher level of consciousness. Sufis do not teach that. They teach that you must come to realization while you're in incarnation and you're using these vehicles. Really, you're never in or out of it, you always are that reality within you. Regardless of how it goes.

The lower mind? We need it, we learn from it. But the higher intelligence only uses the essence of what we learn and what we're doing. We can be trapped in the lower mind, so in so far as the lower mind is concerned, I have some very definite ideas of what should be done with it. Keep it, that's your contact. That's where you learn things. But learn them without being hooked by them, if you can.

That brings us to something Gurdjieff mentioned, and Inayat Khan also mentioned, you've got to **"be in the world, but not of it."** You're doing an act. You know this other part is there. You've had the experience of it. You're lifted up. You're treating everybody with kindness. Maybe they think you're an idiot. To begin with, they think you're foolish to throw out that set of concepts and biases in your mind. If you don't throw them away, how could you do the will of the One? You wouldn't be able to. You'd say this is this, that's that . . . .But if you get to the place where you're really getting it from that, you'll FEEL IT and DO IT. If you don't DO IT when you start getting it, that TOUCH from the INSIDE, that intuitive thing, if you don't follow it out, if you get tricked between that and what your imagination wants, you can imagine something and if you imagine it long enough you say, "Oh, sure, that's coming from the heart." But nine times out of ten, it's your mind working overtime with your particular desire that has manufactured the thing. It's tricky there. You know the only way you find out? When something like that works out and your imagination has worked on you without you being truly hit by your intuition, IT WON'T WORK. If nothing stands in the way of it working, then you know you've tuned into the big-burner. If you tune in on the lesser ones, it won't work. I know a number of young people were sure they knew exactly what they wanted to do. They thought it came from the heart, but it came from the head and from the desires.

Did you ever stop to think in your mind what love is? It really can't be analyzed. You can't lay it out here scientifically and explain it. It's something that hits us. You look and there it is, and if you're getting the feel of it, TAKE IT! It's the most wonderful gift anyone can have. If you don't get the hit from the spiritual heart, as long as you've got the one of your emotional attachment to someone, don't throw it away either. Enjoy it because in the higher octave, you're coming into the love of all and the love of God.

I suppose internationally you might say that Theosophy is dying on the vine. I don't know. I don't think it is here. I don't think Sufism is either. I think it's growing. But so many people just take the words or the intellectual understanding and form a little clique which only they can hang together because, you know, "Only *they* can understand *my* language." That isn't it! It's the OPEN HEART, that's where it is. That's Sufism.

Sam Lewis

Visiting the Dead (Return of Joe Miller)

In June 1990, Joe suffered a serious stroke and was out of action for several months. Remarkably, in October, he re-emerged and ventured downstairs to the lodge to resume his loving harangue of the kids.

Well, this is like visiting the dead, that is myself. Because after people have strokes they have heavy troubles. And I went through 'em, I went through the experience. I had flashes where I couldn't say what I wanted to say. Now there is no one here that isn't aware that normally I can express myself very fully on what I want to say.

Going through this experience, I realized, in my inner consciousness, so much that is true and so wonderful. Things that are there, but that we don't have a language to tell about it. But it is. And it is that wonderful for each and every one of you. All the trials and troubles you have, you know—it ain't there. It's a movie, folks, and we're all in it. We have very good equipment to use. We have a logical mind that can make deductions, that can look at our particular biases and not be stuck on them completely.

I want to tell you something of a humorous nature. I was in my bed at the hospital and I needed to relieve myself. I beat on the bed awhile and I tried the button awhile and nobody came in. So I figured I would sneak down to the foot of the bed and get out. But I found out they had a lot of machinery out there and I fell down and hurt my hip again. I didn't know anything about that, because you see my mind was entirely blacked out for all the time. I was saved from that.

But I figure it this way, if they didn't have in mind me being busy with my kids, you're my kids, I wouldn't be here. So I feel it's kind of my job to tell you as clearly as I believe and I hope that you will all KNOW and REALIZE that you are that REALITY, a part of that reality. And the only reason we don't have our way crawling through life . . . you know, you get an opinion, "Now look, this is the way it's going to be and I don't want to have it happen that way." Well, after a bit, you find out that it's going to happen the way it's going to happen. All of it. But you can have dreams and you can try for them if you want to, but you must have that common sense factor within you. **Common sense? That means have uncommon sense, a sense of who you really are.** When I did find out the one thing, there were moments when I was shivering between "I guess it's me or not me," and "What wasn't me?" I KNOW THAT PART BEYOND US IS IMMORTAL AND EVERY ONE OF YOU SEATED IN THIS ROOM IS IMMORTAL. It's all within you, it's for you to find it and realize it. You say, "Well, I thought this out the best I could and I want to have it this way." Well, I tried that too, but it didn't do me much good and I goofed. I had to work at another direction, then I found out that a lot of things come true partly.

After I came out of it, the first thing I wanted to do was get up to the place where I was living, where my wife was, and I found that I was over here in J.R.'s house on the first floor. They told me I had to be able to walk if I wanted to get up there. Well, you can believe it or not, but I immediately started trying to walk, wobbling on the one leg that I could work at the time.

Whether I could talk or not, once I came into my own house I remembered all the books I studied, all the things that people tell me after you've had a stroke you can't remember, you can but you just won't let go of that part of you that will just let you say that. You have a little trouble that comes with one of these things and mine was with my right hand. And I thought for awhile it didn't belong to me anymore. When I wanted to put my hand in my pocket, it would slide down. When I talked to the therapist, I found out that's one of the first things you have to learn about after you've had a stroke. So I did a little thinking in my own mind, this arm is a part of me, it's a part of everything. It's still a little bit screwy, but so far, it's started out all right.

Within us, individually, is the responsibility for this vehicle that we are carrying. And so, it can help each part, or be the opposite. You could meditate long enough, not go anywhere, not eat, and after awhile you'd stop ticking. Other than that they let you play your own games. But there is something inside you right now that KNOWS the truth. If I could find it out, with my phony hand that wouldn't behave itself, you can. I know gradually I'll get it together. I never stopped to think of it that way before. I thought, "Well, this is just the body, I AM IN HERE." Is that so? Yeah, "I" is in there. That egotistical bastard that don't use even a little common sense. Think about it.

Look at your own ideas and biases. Look deep into them. Look at the truth that's in there. You've got the truth inside of you. When you came here, you had something particular to do and find in your adventures. Sure, but you've got free will. You can climb trees or anything you want to. But it's real. I've been into some of it, I don't know a great deal from there, but inside of me, in my consciousness itself, I can't say it to you in magic words so that you could have it. Everybody has to find it in themselves, and start living it. Of course, the principle I work with is more or less in that direction. Believe it or not, I love everybody sitting in this room. I love everybody. I've always been that way, I'm a little nuts. But I like it that way.

You can allow something in your life to leave you preoccupied for years and years and you might miss that wonderful thing that is the real you trying to express itself. This is what I'm trying to say. I know it sounds strange, but you've heard me give talks for a long time and you know I mean it, I'm not kidding. It's wonderful. So I figured what I could do is yak at you kids as much as I could to bring them to an understanding of that. I don't care what title you put on it. But feel it. I wanted to tell you how very much I love you. Sitting in my house, it worried me to come down here. I wondered if you would have the feeling that I know comes from you when I'm talking to you. If that was lost, I wouldn't want be living any longer. It's because of the people I love that I want to carry on.

Broadcast from the Trees (Joe's Last Rap)

This excerpt is from a brief talk given in June, 1992 at one of the annual "Sufi Camp-Outs" that Joe's friend, Yakin, organized in Portola State Park. Joe loved the setting, with its tall redwoods. It was Joe's last rap before he fell. It was clear that something would happen soon. Joe was getting very frail and seemed almost translucent.

I see more of you here already. That is, more than I can see, I see. Do you understand what I'm saying? I don't know what the hell I'm talking about, but you get the idea.

It's so **beautiful** here. Certainly, a blessing on this land is here. I've thought of these places, but I've been far away. I always remember this temple.

We've got a lot of beautiful things, where we come from, where we live. We've got a lot of blessings. Of course, we don't think much about our blessings. Hell, no. "We don't have . . . ." Forget it. You've got to think of your blessings and really feel they are blessings and let 'em flow out from you. Let people feel them. MAKE 'EM FEEL IT! Then what you feel inside, they'll feel it too. If you give them love, THEY'LL FEEL LOVE.

It isn't just "Well, I don't know whether I should be allowed to think that way, because my mind can't . . . ." Oh, horse manure. Come on, get with it. Go, go, go, that's the idea. FEEL IT! Keep living. I've gone into some places where they were so quiet, I think they figured you better not move anything because you might break it. Well, not only make it, but BREAK IT, MOVE IT!

Everybody's squawking about this western world. We're in it! We're in the middle of it. And we've been played as the chumps for it or otherwise. But you can only breathe for yourself. Feel the fullness of life. **When you look up there and see that sky and that sun and those gorgeous trees that have been here for thousands of years watching you . . . .I wish we could have a broadcast from the trees themselves to give an opinion of us. 'Cause we're midgets in one way, but not in another. You feel loose. You can loosen it up a little. But you got to realize in seriousness this isn't the end! We've been here hundreds and thousands of times. We've been here before.** Start realizing that this is only one of many lives, countless, in fact. FEEL INTO

IT!

Come on, we've got stuff inside of us, too. We don't have to have other people hitch you up. We can think about it ourselves and feel it and be it. If you're worrying about hurting your face by letting it get wrinkles, remember that it takes less lines to make a smile then a frown. So smile, keep smiling. Just feel it deep inside, feel it right now in your hearts and in your beings and KNOW what this is! Look through it all. We're all through it all, everyone is all through it all, in every direction. Come on, we gotta shake it loose and get with it! You've got to do it by your own efforts, no one can do it for you. They can tell you about it, but you have to make it happen.

LIVE FOR YOURSELF! WHY NOT? Even an old fossil like me, with one foot in the grave and the other on a banana peel. I'm enjoying my life. And after the things I've seen . . . .Well, I've seen it all. I like it and I'm going to take the trip again. In fact, as soon as I can get it, I'll take it when I get there. I got friends here and I'm going to keep on seeing them. I'll be there. This is not just for this time, this is a proposition that you signed for all ETERNITY and swell on into Eternity, breathe, live a little of the other part!

Rumi said, "Ours is not a caravan of despair." Remember that, will ya? There are points when we may be in the dumps, but you can be out of it and feel that lightness and live. Each of us creates our own atmosphere. You have to feel it for yourself.

I see a lot of people here that I've known from before. So many times I don't even remember what their names are. BUT I KNOW 'EM. I've been here for so damn long I feel like Santa Claus. And remember, Santa Claus always was there.

Allah Bismallah
Say that God is One
Living, eternal, and beside Him none

Be loose as a goose. Hang loose. What the hell. It'll last longer, much longer. Believe me when I say I'm in my eighty-eighth year and I'm having fun and I love life and it's jumping. So let's all have it jumping. No sad-sack business about it. **Shake it up.** I can't make you think, but it's damned easy to make you feel. So adjust the feeling part. You can just add a little thinking along with it, out at the edges. But the feeling is the main thing, that's what makes the world go around.

On the walk

A group in front of the Lodge

Joe and Guin with "Lamala"
(Lama Dudjom Dorje)

Joe, Guin , Lance (Guin's brother),
and Richard Power

PART TWO:

Rolling the Wonder Bread Truck and Other Amazements

Editor's Note:
What Joe Saw From the Outhouse

In Part II, Joe offers glimpses into his early life. He talks about his parents, his childhood, some psychic experiences, going into show business, and getting married. He tells of joining the Theosophical Society as well as other groups, and shares his encounters with Annie Besant and Dr. W.Y. Evans-Wentz.

Truth has a human face. Joe wasn't able or even inclined to reject the western lifestyle for the path of the sannyasin. His lot was that of a householder and a laborer trying to understand the daily grind as a test and a learning process. He made his way in show business as a tenor and a comic in vaudeville and burlesque, then later, as an agent for the Entertainer's Union. He worked odd-jobs when he had to—truck-driver, house painter, coppersmith in the shipyards, night manager in a seedy cinema. Joe went through the women on the chorus lines. He married four times. He lost his first brood of children in divorce, then later raised a second set who had no interest in his passion for life's spiritual dimension. Along the way, he suffered and caused suffering and gained an intimate understanding of the whole deranged pattern of human ignorance that he often referred to as "the manure that makes the flowers grow."

Long before the Flower Children of the 1960's started turning on to LSD, Ravi Shankar, and the Joshua Light Show, Joe Miller was fooling around with color and music, seeking to unlock their occult powers to heal and enlighten. Long before the Whole Life Expo crammed the Moscone Center with rune stones, healing crystals, aura cleansings, pagan rites, and channelings of St. Germain, Joe Miller was exploring sex magic in Aleister Crowley's school and listening to Guy Ballard's sales pitch about the hidden masters of Mount Shasta.

During the 1930's and 1940's, Joe traveled around the country, doing gigs in hick towns and big cities. Wherever he went, Joe looked up bold mystics, charlatans, quacks, and true-blue experimenters, getting glimpses of inventions like the "Clauvilux" and the "Luxatone," color organs that could allegedly alter a person's psychic or physical condition, and collecting other arcane lore. Throughout Joe's flat, buried away in his steamer trunk, stuffed behind his bookcases, shoved underneath his bed, I found the evidence of his explorations—prisms of all shapes and sizes, rose-tinted sunglasses, colored light bulbs, and little booklets from various groups claiming to explain the hidden mysteries.

Joe's awakening deepened and ripened throughout his life from the ruby magenta glow of the wood stove that he saw from his baby walker through the scent of sandalwood rising on Lake Minnetonka to his ecstatic communing with the dawn on the rooftops of downtown San Francisco. Joe's accidental meeting with Annie Besant, and her later remarks concerning his future, gave him a great lift. But it was over twenty years later, through his encounter with Dr. W.Y. Evans-Wentz, that Joe received verification that he had found the motherlode and a new era of his life began to unfold. Of all those he had met in the West, Evans-Wentz considered Joe "the only person to understand the theories of the Clear Light of Reality."

The story of how Joe progressed from his fascination with the occult power of color and music to the "Doctrine of the Clear Light," from "astral real estate" to the nitty gritty, isn't about how someone "attained something." It's a tale of unfolding. "Life itself is the teacher," Joe said. "I surrender to the love of the One which teaches me from within."

One night, when Joe was twelve years old, he went to the outhouse. Looking up at the dark sky, he saw what seemed to be two vast human figures outlined in the stars, a male and female in coitus. He felt he had seen something sacred and mysterious. Many years later, he understood the epiphany better when he came across the following footnote:

> Visualize the energizing aspect of the cosmos as being the divine father (Tib. Yab) and the intellectual aspect as the divine mother (Tib. Yum). Think of them as being in union and inseparably one. Realization of this divine at-one-ment is the goal, the Great Symbol.

> *Tibetan Book of Yoga and Secret Doctrine*, p. 147.

On one level, Joe's anecdote tells of a young boy's awakening sexuality. On another, it is the tale of a being, with many lifetimes of questing behind him, receiving a message. At the age of twelve, Joe had a vision in the outhouse. Half a century later, in his talks, the balancing of polarities was a profound and recurrent theme—Yab/Yum, Siva/Sakti, Truth/ Love, Heart/Mind, Form/Formlessness, Light/Darkness, Unity/Uniqueness.

Forty Below Zero

I was born January 20th, 1904, in Minneapolis, Minnesota, at 3:10 in the morning. It was forty below zero.

The doctor told my father, "Do you want me to save your wife or the child?" Now the old man being WHOLE HOG said, "I want you to save both of 'em." But the doctor said, "It would be better if we didn't try. The child's too big." Anyway, they managed it. I got in all right, and I weighed fifteen pounds.

When I was born, I had a veil, that's sort of an extra bag of skin over the head. It's something that the spiritualists go for quite a bit. It's supposed to have psychic importance. But neither my mom nor my dad paid much attention to it.

My father was the only one in his family born with one, my mother was the only child in her family born with one, and I was the only one in ours. They say if you keep it and pickle it, they can tell you how your life will work out. Well, we didn't pickle it.

Mom And Dad

The old man was a drunk. But he also had a good mind.

We were poor. We didn't get the kind of clothes or grub that the other kids got. I knew it too. At Christmas, everybody would get together, and I could see that our relatives were awful fat and we were awful lean.

The old man was smarter than all of 'em. He'd start talking and put them in a hole right away. Still, they had steady jobs and we didn't even know if we'd get shoes or not.

For a little thumbnail sketch of my father's background, his life started out with someone kidnapping him from home because he was an acrobat and could do all kinds of tricks. They stole him away and put him in the circus. He went along and learned the painting trade. He stayed on a bit with the circus and did the high trapeze.

Then all of a sudden, he got religion. He went into the Salvation Army. When he was a kid he had only two months of schooling. It ended when they tried to teach him the catechism and he threw the slate at the teacher's head. Anyway, when he joined the Salvation Army, he had to learn the Bible word by word.

In those days, you also had to learn a musical instrument to join the Salvation Army. He picked the trumpet. Dad became a captain. They gave him transportation out from West Virginia to Minnesota and that's where he met my mother. He came to her door, begging for the Salvation Army, you know, "Got any old clothes . . . ."

My mother's grandfather was a sea captain who settled in Minnesota and bought some good property. Her father blew his inheritance on race horses and bad investments. He married a girl of sixteen and the children just kept coming. I ended up with seven or eight aunts and uncles. His money just went. So he got very dramatic and instead of keeping his connections to the higher social strata where he could make a living, he went out to do it the hard way and started digging sewers. So what happened? He had a heart attack.

My father had Dutch blood. My mother was of English and Scottish extraction. One of my dad's people got dressed up for the Boston Tea Party. My mother's great-grandparents were massacred by Indians. So, as you can see, I've got revolutionaries on one side, and pioneer stock on the other.

By the time I was eleven or twelve, my mother and father were talking to me as if I were a grown-up. By that time, my old man was very much a socialist. My mother was very religious, "faith the size of a mustard seed" and so forth.

When the old man got stiff and didn't come home on a Saturday night or blew all the money he made, why my mother would just say, "I have faith it will all be okay." Now the old man had been in the Salvation Army, so he could quote scripture right and left, whenever it was suitable. He would say that there is a statement to the effect that a man is saved by the faith of his wife. My mom would answer, "Well, then you'll be saved Lan, 'cause I have perfect faith that everything will be all right." Meanwhile, at that time, we didn't have any shoes.

I loved them both very much. I feel no animosity at all. I thought my father was very good in the head, and my mother was very good in the heart. So I got something from both sides.

As far as schooling, I got to the eighth grade. The folks didn't have the money to support me going any farther.

I wasn't very big for my age, but I went down and tried to volunteer for military service. I wanted to ride one of those horses. They still had cavalry in the 1st World War. But the guy said, "Go home and wait."

The old man went merrily on his way, drinking, going fishing, quoting the *Bible* when he got stiff. He worked as a paper-hanger and painter. Same as Hitler. I learned the trade too.

We lived in the suburbs of Minneapolis. He could have had a great business. But he'd be working along and I'd be working with him and then he'd say, "Well look, let's go fishing." Geez, you got these people's house all broke up, you got furniture piled everywhere, half a room is painted or half has got wallpaper on it. He says, "I gotta go fishing." So what do you do? He's your father, so you go fishing.

I Found Out I Could Sing

I found out I could sing. I also found out I could make a buck singing. So I worked the amateur shows. Things got better for me once I got into show business. It was exciting, although it was a hell of a precarious living.

If you got into vaudeville, the ordinary people thought, "Wow! This is a big deal. Wonderful. The guy's wearing a tuxedo." Maybe it's the only time he wears it, maybe it's second-hand.

Of course, my mother's family (my aunts and uncles) didn't think too much of that. They were strictly square—the kind that went to work in the post office and got to be the local postmaster after twenty years.

I first found out I could sing when I was knee-high to a grasshopper, so they had me and another kid sing in the local church.

Meanwhile, the old man and I would be working in a joint, wall-papering the place and he'd say, "Joe, what the hell, give us a song." So I would sing "Irish Eyes Are Smiling" or "A Little Bit Of Heaven."

Once when I was singing that way there was a sick guy in the other room. Afterward, he told his daughter that he was going to commit suicide until he heard me singing. Even much later in life, at the "Gay Nineties" nightclub, before I retired, people would come up and say, "There's a certain something in your voice." And I would say, "Yeah. It's just that I'm a tenor and I'm louder than the rest." But, nevertheless, without any specific personalization or particularization on my part, some of these things have occurred. It happens to everybody. **Whether you know it or not, you become an instrument, or a lens for that ray of Light, if you want to put it in terms of color. After all, if it's all One anyhow, we only think we're making the decisions.**

But, nevertheless, it has always been my dedication that the singing be used in that way—for helping people. And when I worked in the burlesque houses, kids would come up to me with a problem or some question, and I would pat them on the back. I would rub their bellies and try to help them straighten it out.

Psychic Experiences

As a young man, I would often have precognition, but not consciously. I'd dream of a certain situation, with me in it. No ideas about such a situation coming up or the people in it. Not even making any particular connection of importance with the dream itself until the experience was actually happening. Then I'd say, "Yeah, wow, I dreamt this."

I got a job in a musical stock company and they decided they were going to put on "The Student Prince." They figured they'd have some guy, a student from the University, sing the lead in it. I was in a quartet in the show. It ended up that they gave me the lead for two weeks. My salary was sixty-seven dollars a week.

The first night we put it on, I was right in the middle of this song and the precognition thing hit! Jesus, yeah. You got people sitting up there, the chorus and all. The character is thinking of the days gone by and how much he's in love with the heroine and he is making a gesture with a glass. All dressed up, fancy. Then ZUNK! Right in the middle of it, it hit me, "Yeah, I dreamt this part." In other words, it wasn't important when I dreamt it. But when it happened, I made the connection.

From my point of view, anything that you get through your senses, whether it's called ESP or not, is a matter of your own projection, something that you've dug out of your own consciousness. But then if there is any validity to any of it, this is all One Consciousness anyway and we're just like bubbles on it.

Once I was driving an oldsmobile in St. Louis. I had been back East. It was wet pavement, and my first wife was with me. We had the two kids in the car. I had been driving for a long time.

I said, "Well, you drive for awhile." So she got in behind the wheel just outside of Columbus, Missouri. She was going around a curve. Now when she first started driving, I said, "Now look, if it ever starts skidding or something, don't put your foot on the brake and if you get off on the side, don't jerk it out, stop and start in low, gradually get out of it when no cars are coming." But she was rather impulsive. So the car started to slide off the side and she jerked it one way and I said, "Give it a pull the other way!" And we're on this wet pavement and a Greyhound bus comes up on the car. Bus and car meet. Very unhappy for the car, not a scratch on the bus.

When it hit, I was holding one baby in my arms. I got a cut, the baby got a cut across the head. They took us right to the hospital. The bus driver looks at me. I said, "Well, when will you be going through Columbus again?" He said the same time next day. All I needed was a patch on my nose and a couple of stitches and I went back to the hotel. Meanwhile, my mother was home in Minnesota, taking a nap and it's in the afternoon. She jumps up and says to my father, "Lan, Joe and his wife and babies were just in an accident. I don't think it's fatal or anything."

Later, when I got home, we checked the time, it was the same.

There was a similar incident involving my sister and brother. Al was out of town. He was in North Dakota on the bum, walking through the mud all night. Next morning, my sister woke up and said, "I've been walking through the mud all night." She was just dreaming, she thought. We didn't know where Al was at the time. But later, we found out that he was in those exact circumstances that night.

Now was one thinking of the other so strongly that they got the transmission, like on a radio? And if so, which one was it? Or, was it a matter of both of 'em thinking in the same way on the same level and getting a feel for it, the same vibe? Either way, it's all consciousness.

In one sense, it's all a game, it's all an illusion. But you can't tell that to a group, really. You can't bring that to them too strongly because it ruins everything they've got going. It's all an illusion. But if a certain part of the illusion is important for them in making a better life, what are you going to do? Pull it out from under them? You just don't do that.

It isn't that you think, "I don't do that." There is just a monitor in there. It's not separate from yourself. But you know better than you know. Really. It's like something else is functioning and yet still it's you, and yet, it's not. Wow!

The clear awareness isn't anything to look up to or down to. It's just the way it goes. Some people enjoy trying to tear down something for someone else and use that sort of technique. But I don't. I figure you can catch more flies with molasses than vinegar.

It's not any conceit on my part because it's not something that I make a judgment on. It's just what comes out. If you just leave yourself in AT-ONE-MENT and get the feel of it, you know what you can do and what you can't do. It's the same as when you're working in the theatre and you're the straight man in the act. You've got this regular line or piece of business you do, but depending upon the feel of the audience, there is something that automatically functioning from inside you. And no credit is due to any particular analysis or anything else on your part.

It's something that happens that you don't learn, you just sort of fall into it. That's the way I look at it. But this is a happiness—*to try it*. It's joyous, not sad-sack.

It's so simple. It can't be explained.

Wonder Bread

My first wife's mother was pretty sharp and she said, "Oh, actors don't amount to anything and you're not good enough anyway. Why don't you get a job doing something else?" So I took a job driving a truck for Wonder Bread, and I got along all right.

I heard the "Wonder Bakers," a musical advertisement on the radio, and I said, "Why not put this thing out locally and build up business for selling bread in the different stores?" So we did. We got a little organ, one that you could fold up. I got another singer a job too. We would go around and sing. Finally, we rented the biggest theatre in town, had a big parade, took out a full-page ad and put it on.

But Wonder Bread's advertising company said, "Yeah, we'll use the promotion, but not them. We're the advertising company. You allocate a million dollars a year to us." They tried to put it on in other places, but they didn't have the stuff, like timing, that people with background in show business have, so it wasn't successful.

So there I was, selling Wonder Bread and working the nightclubs after dark. Now, that's a hell of a combination. I'd log about a hundred twenty miles a day then go spend three or four hours in a nightclub. I would squeeze in some time between jobs.

One fine, snowy morning I went to sleep at the wheel, drove the truck off the road and turned it over. I had some nice flat loaves of bread in the back of the truck afterward. I didn't hurt myself at all. I just woke up and the truck was on its side. I turned off the motor. I could look back and see how I went off the road gradually.

The little guy in charge of the trucks came out and said, "Well look, these trucks are expensive. If you're sleepy, get out and hammer on the engine or relieve yourself or something." He told me he had heard I was holding down two jobs and that I had to decide on one or the other.

The bread truck paid more, so I quit the nightclub.

Wonder was the first big corporation to take over bread nationally. They'd buy up the little bakeries. But they didn't want you to buy any other bread if you worked there. If they heard you bought any other kind of bread at home, you were in bad with them. In other words, they didn't just want you for the hours that you worked, they wanted devotees. If you went out for entertainment, they wanted you to go play bridge with the other truckers and their wives.

When the Depression hit, I went on relief. After awhile, I got an offer to go sing in Chicago. Music, entertainment, always seemed to fall into my lap. It didn't fall in gracefully or make me a lot of loot, but whenever things got tough that door would open for me.

No Creed And No Doctrine

The very first book I read on Theosophy, I found at the public library. It was Annie Besant's *Ancient Wisdom*. [22] Someone had misplaced it. It was on the Psychology shelf.

The Theosophical Society was then just as it is now. It had never been very big there in Minneapolis, but the folks that were in it all got old and died off. Some people had started a new one, a little nucleus of a few people. I've never been in any lodge that was real big. It's always been just a little seed.

After I joined, I had some psychic experiences—like seeing huge figures in black and white—what I thought to be the Great Ones. As I figure it now, it was strictly a projection from my mind. I would look and see something like a black and white drawing of faces outside the window or against the wall.

I didn't believe with a fanatical belief. "This is possible, anything is possible," was more my attitude. I was fascinated by it all. I didn't realize that in setting up a concept like that of a hierarchy, you're setting up a dictatorial thing and it's held to a certain pattern in time and space. I didn't realize this at that point.

The people in the T.S. were pretty uptight about just the words. The Scandinavian people in the Minneapolis T.S. during that period were very religious, so they'd take the word that was written as pure doctrine. "It's gotta be just this way!" Stand by authority . . . .

They organized this proposition, the T.S., so that people would be able to see through the particular religion they were in and then see how they could get to a point where they could FALL AWAKE and know what it's all about.

As far as this particular society, the San Francisco lodge, is concerned, we're not plugging any particular religion. Any particular religion you're in, if it's doing it for you, stay with it. If it isn't doing it for you, that's another story. You have to use your judgment then.

Two ideas were spread by Theosophy: REINCARNATION and KARMA. If there is anything that Theosophy has done, it's spread those two ideas.

After all, at the establishment of the Society, the Chief, the Boss, told the two masters, Moria and Koot Humi, who were supposed to be the inspiration, that it would be all right if they wanted to start the T.S., but that whether it would go for better than a hundred-year cycle was problematical.

In other words, it sort of took on the job of spreading these two concepts, reincarnation and karma, more fully in the West. This it has done. Now, whether it can adjust to the set-up today and how the kids look at it now is a different thing. In our particular lodge, we're trying to express the OPENESS and the NO CREED and NO DOCTRINE idea of finding out for themselves.

I had ambition and I thought I would pour it into the Theosophical Society. Even while I was working in nightclubs, I thought, "Well, when the time comes and I retire, geez, I can use all the advertising, all the ideas I learned from show business to promote this thing." Then I realized that ain't it. You can't. Those that are ready for it are going to come to it. Oh, you could push a lot of them in, but they'd fall out just as quickly. Because you would be using the same kind of technique that you would use in selling them anything.

Those that got connected with the T.S. have always added up to just enough to keep it going. Just enough. No more. When one goes down maybe another one pops up someplace else . . . .But there is always somebody around saying, "Well, can't we organize this and make it a set thing?" THE MINUTE THEY MAKE IT SET, IT'S SOUR. Bound to be. How the hell is the life in it going to get out? Everything we are is all movement anyway, so it's going to crack the shell sooner or later.

Sandalwood On Lake Minnetonka

After I joined the Theosophical Society, I was visiting a friend of mine back in Minnesota, on Lake Minnetonka. We were walking along and went into some trees. I smelled incense, sandalwood incense. But there was nothing like sandalwood anywhere near there. Then I just took a gentle, in-drawn breath and was filled with ECSTASY.

At that time, I was working in a nightclub and driving a bakery truck too, so I probably had myself honed down pretty fine from the actual work I was doing. But I wanted to feel it again, I wanted that feeling that you couldn't exactly say was a feeling. It was an ecstasy.

And I wasn't thinking about anything. It was just a gentle breath. It was there because I was still enough, without anything bothering the conscious mind. So it just happened.

Well, it was about two years before it happened again. I wanted it to come back so much, I cried. And then it happened again without trying. It was just a happening. And I wanted to find out what it was. I even cried that it had come back. **It's like pleasure and pain mixed. You couldn't call it pleasure, you couldn't call it pain.** It was just an ecstasy.

After awhile, I got so that I could just do it with a gentle, in-drawn breath. But it wasn't me. It's just tuning into the THATNESS, the IT-ness, God, love, whatever you want to call it. The name you put on it doesn't make any difference. It's the experience.

So I can sit here now and just draw on a gentle breath. I wouldn't dare breathe that way all the time because I wouldn't want to be walking that high off the ground. But I can sit down and be very quiet and it happens. **It's just an ecstasy in the very air.**

First Ray Invocation

After I moved to Chicago, I got a little better in show business and started working with an important guy named Paul Ash. We were working the Oriental Theatre. Before going to the show, I would spend some time at the Liberal Catholic Church. They had a little meditation. It appealed to me very much.

I had tried to become a priest in the LCC, but the guy in charge said, "Well, you can't be working down at the burlesque house and be a priest in the Liberal Catholic Church. I don't think people would go for it."

The first time I heard the *First Ray Invocation*, which I've used for many years now, was in 1924. Annie Besant came to town. It was to be the first time we were to see the LCC service. They put it on in a big hall.

Now, in the LCC, just as in the Roman Catholic Church, women couldn't be inside the sanctuary while a service was underway. So when they called Annie Besant in for the snapper, she just walked up in front of the rail to read this *First Ray Invocation*:

> May the holy ones show us the light we seek, and give us the strong aid of their compassion and their wisdom.
> There is a peace that passeth all understanding. It abides in the hearts of those who live in the eternal.
> There is a power that maketh all things new, and it lives and moves in those who know the self as One.
> May that peace brood over us and that power uplift us until we stand where the one initiator is invoked, until we see that star shine forth.

I said, "Wow, I gotta learn this!" And I did. But, in those days, no one was supposed to use it unless they were a priest in the LCC. Well, naturally, when I heard that I knew immediately that I was going to learn it and use it.

There was another line that I dropped. I didn't like the feel of it. It sounded like you should grovel. It seemed a bit slavish to me, so I just cut it out. It went, "May the holy ones whose disciples we aspire to be . . . ." I just figure that if the desire is there, the aspiration, then you're IN, and there's no auditions.

Of Worldly Jewels and Riches

I kept going down to this church and meditating. But I wouldn't call it meditation as such. I was just going to be in the atmosphere of the place. I liked the feel of it.

One day, this guy with an outfit on comes in with a procession behind him. It was Krishnamurti [23]. I thought, "I gotta be getting down to the theatre, and this is obviously something I shouldn't be in on." Hell, I had just joined the Theosophical Society.

I walked across the hall to the elevator, and this little old lady is standing there. It was Annie Besant [24]. I went up to her and said, "Hi, my name is Joe Miller." And she said, "Well, glad to know you." I said, "This is the happiest moment of my life."

When I had seen her speak back in Minneapolis, you couldn't even get near her.

Annie Besant and I went into the library and talked. She said there was something special going on in there with Krishnamurti. I looked at the time, I had to get back to the theatre.

Next morning, I went down to the T.S., looking at the books, then on to the theatre. After the first show, I went on to the LCC and the library there. They said, "We were looking all over for you." Now, with my logical mind, I thought, "If all these psychic powers were there, why the hell wouldn't they have known I was on the next block at the T.S.?"

They said, "Annie Besant wanted to see you before she left for New York and India." Ah, man. Pow! I was built up by that.

I said to myself, "Well, maybe now I can become a priest in the LCC here in Chicago." I went to see the Bishop. He said, "No, I can't make you a priest. But I talked your case over with Dr. Besant. She said you have some other work to do." Bang! Swelled me up great.

I went home that night and had a dream. I didn't see anything at all, I just heard a voice. It said, "What has Annie Besant done for the world? Look at all these buildings . . . ." and so forth. Then I answered, "She has built spiritual structures far greater than these physical ones."

I decided that if she wanted to talk to me, I'd write her a letter. In it, I told her if there was anything she wanted me to do, she should just tell me. I finished it up with a postscript, a bit of corn that came to me:

Of wordly jewels and riches, I have none.
My strength of will surpasses all.
Thine not mine be done.

It just popped in.

I got a letter from a guy travelling with her. He described the route they were going to take across Russia and then on to India and Adyar. He said Annie Besant wanted to know how far I was in the "Inner School." You're supposed to be a member for three years and then they give you a bunch of phony books. Already, even at that point, I was against it. I definitely felt—LEAVE IT OPEN! If someone isn't ready for it they can't dig it anyway, regardless of how hard you try to tell them.

Eventually, this guy who wrote the letter came through Minneapolis. I went up to him and said, "I got your letter. But what did Annie Besant say?" His response was, "She said as far as you were concerned that when the time came you would know what you were supposed to do."

I couldn't go wrong with that, I'll go for that. It made sense. It seemed logical. It satisfied a certain part, too.

Ruby Magenta (The Earliest I Remember . . .)

The earliest I remember is being in a baby walker. I couldn't have been more than one year old. We were living in Minnesota where it's very cold. They had one of those air-tight stoves, just metal. You keep putting fuel in it and it gets hot enough to warm the joint. There were a couple of rooms in the place.

The stove had a sort of ruby magenta spot on it from the heat. And my mom and dad had gone into the next room. My father had said, "Now, Joey, don't touch it!" Of course, they had no sooner left the room than I pushed my walker over and put my hand on the red spot. It just fascinated me. It was so beautiful.

I closed my hand. I remember my thoughts at that time, "Don't tell 'em." I couldn't do anything to double-cross the beautiful thing I had seen. So I kept my hands closed. That night, as my mother was putting me to bed, she pried open my hand and there I had the blisters.

That was my first experience with color that meant something.

Years later, in about 1940, I was experimenting with a prism. Normally, when you look through a prism, it's broken up into the warm side and the cool side—the red, orange and yellow and the blue, indigo and violet. You don't even see the green.

But I found that when you hold it up and look at light through it, you get a break of another color than you get if you just shine a light through it. In other words, you get a point where the red and violet come together.

It gives you a ruby magenta.

Later, I read that Goethe had done a discourse on color and said that Newton didn't give all that was in the spectrum because he didn't make a complete circle with it. Then I saw the picture of the front cover of C.W. Leadbeater's *Masters of the Path*, showing the Buddha seated and all the colors coming out from him, like the bands of the aura.

Also, when it was slow in show business, I'd get out in the frosty air and look at the sun. If it was cloudy enough that the sun didn't hurt my eyes, I'd sometimes see an effect similar to what you see with an electric light bulb—the colors breaking from it prismatically. Of course, maybe there was just something wrong with my eyes. But my practical experience led me to believe that there was something to all of this.

What struck me about color is that it's just about the subtlest thing I could contact physically. I found out that people were interested in correlating color and music for healing. This triggered the idea that since I knew about the music, I should go find someone who knew about the color.

The Clauvilux and the Luxatone

I was in Minneapolis when I heard that a guy by the name of Thomas Wilford had tried to put together a "color organ" in New York. I figured, "Well, I gotta work in a few theatres and try to get them to book me in a New York club."

I was in burlesque at the time. I got to Chicago, then I got booked into Detroit. From Detroit, I got booking into Buffalo. From Buffalo, I got in touch with an agent in New York City and he booked me into the "Irving Place," which was in a tough neighborhood. In fact, the club was run by four gangsters. They warned me, "Now look, don't make any passes at the chorus line. If you do, you're gonna get hurt."

After I got settled in the job, I called Thomas Wilford's office. They said he had concerts on such and such a night for kids going to school. I went. It was on one of the upper floors of the Grand Central Theatre building. They had overstuffed chairs, double-arm width.

You sit there. You're in a complete blackout, no light leaking in from anywhere. There is a wide screen. Wilford would play his organ and the colors would come on the screen.

Naturally, I wanna yak with the guy. So I wrote him a note and put my phone number on it. I was staying at a funny place where a bunch of performers lived. Wilford called me and I went to see him.

He explained that he had tried to correlate color with music. He had worked with one or two large symphony orchestras. If he put up a big enough screen to show the colors the way he wanted, the music just seemed like an accompaniment. On the other hand, if he put in too much music and not enough color that didn't work either. He was selling little cabinets that would go through the sequence of changes in color and geometrical designs. Those sold for a couple hundred bucks each. That would be about fifteen hundred dollars nowadays.

So much for Wilford. I realized he hadn't worked it out.

Meanwhile, I wrote to Spencer Lewis out in San Jose. I joined the Ancient Mystical Order Of Rosicrucians to get their literature. In one of his magazine articles, Lewis said that he had a "Luxatone," and claimed that this contraption correlated color and music. So I wrote to him to make an appointment for a year later 'cause I figured I could get out to the coast by then.

Spencer Lewis had started out with correspondence courses and built it all up from there. He used a kind of coercion through which he tried to attract people. In some of the first papers you sign, you say something like, "Well now, if I don't stay with this group may all the horrible entities of the astral plane tear me to pieces bit by bit." It worked. But not on me. I don't like to be fenced in.

In 1935, I got out to the West Coast and landed a job working seven nights a week at Eddie Spolak's burlesque house. There was a certain date that I was to have an appointment with the guy, so on that day, I went down to Greyhound and said, "Give me a ticket to San Josie." The guy shook his head and said, "Look, here in California, J is pronounced H." Anyway, I got there.

Now the pictures in the magazine made the place seem tremendous, as huge as the Taj Mahal. But when I got there, I saw that it was all confined within a city block. His secretary said, "Well, I don't know, he's just had some dental work done." I said, "I traveled out here from New York. I got this letter a year ago, I want to see him."

Finally, Spencer Lewis showed up. In his pictures he seemed like a huge guy. It must have been the angles at which the shots were taken. In the pictures, he looked as if he were a nice, fat six foot tall. But, actually, he was a little short guy.

When I saw Lewis, I realized he had just had all his teeth pulled out. I thought that was kind of strange. If he were as great, as important and as capable as the build-up made it seem, what did he have to lose his teeth for? According to the lessons I had read, it oughta have been easy for him to have whatever kind of body he wanted and to have his teeth the way he wanted.

He sat down behind his desk and indicated a chair for me. My chair was at a lower level. In other words, it's the old psychological trick—when you talk to him, you've got to look up at him.

He said, "Okay, whaddya want? I'm not feeling so good." I said, "I can see that." So I quoted from a particular lesson number from his own correspondence course and asked him why he couldn't have used the powers mentioned. He didn't like that, he just said, "So whaddya want to see me for?"

I said, "I wrote you concerning the Luxatone, the color organ you have functioning here. I wrote you from New York, concerning Thomas Wilford and his Clauvilux."

"Well, I'll tell you," he answered. "We got a thing hooked up that we got some music out of and some color out of but there really wasn't much sense to it so after awhile we just tore it down." In other words, you really couldn't do anything specifically with it, you couldn't adjust it for healing or changing people's atttitudes. "There's only one thing that I saw happen in color and music," he continued. "One of my children was playing the piano, the other was playing the cello, I was painting, I was working with silver on the canvas. When they struck a certain note in the piece they were playing, the silver went all over and covered the whole canvas, without any doing on my part. That's all I can tell you."

So I thanked him very much, left the joint and, of course, dropped my membership. I figured, "Well, if this guy doesn't know any more than that, he's not going to help me a whole hell of a lot."

My Worst Christmas

I'll tell you about my worst Christmas.

I was in L.A. I had applied for a job and I went out to visit my aunt and uncle, thinking I could horn in on a Christmas dinner. But when I got out there to see them, they said "Well, Joe, we're glad to see you, but we're going out to Christmas dinner with friends."

I didn't have a nickel. I had to get myself back downtown. I did have a room in a boarding house. I was waiting to hear whether or not I would get this job.

When I got back downtown, I looked through all of my clothes, and I found fifteen cents. At that time, you could get a box of soda crackers for a nickel and you could buy a dime's worth of cheese. I thought of all the time I had lived up to then, I was only thirty-five years old.

You'd be surprised at the thoughts that ran through my mind that night. My pillow was wet when I went to sleep. However, it didn't work out too bad. Next day, a letter arrived with a check for one hundred dollars in it, then I got the job I wanted and everything was okay.

Before the Eyes Can See

I had a wife and two children. The little girl loved the fat, and the boy only ate the lean. We had great times together 'cause I was like a kid with 'em. We lived in Chicago and I worked in Detroit. I had to commute back and forth. So there I am in Detroit, doing what I can to make it and she's back in Chicago. I took the day off and went back. I had been tipped off that she was playing around with somebody else. Of course, I had been doing the same thing with entire chorus lines.

When I got to the front door, there is a rumbling inside. Then, I go to the back door and there's a guy going down the steps. Oh, I got so sentimental. I started thinking about the children and about her. Wow. Attachment so strong. So I go back to Detroit. I heard she took a trip from Minneapolis to Detroit with a gangster and saw the show I was doing. Then she met someone with a lot of money. She sold him a bill of goods that she really isn't what she is. She convinced him that she's a very gentle, agreeable, shrinking vine type.

The divorce papers she had made up claimed "desertion." I got her to sign a paper that said I wouldn't contest it if she changed it to "incompatibility." The divorce went through and I moved to California. Then they sent me a notice that they wanted to adopt the children, but the notice wasn't sent from Chicago until three days after I would have had to notify them, or I couldn't do anything about it. So I never saw the kids again.

I had to go through another marriage before the sentimentality part broke down. In that second one, I had an adopted son, and another son and daughter of my own.

I had come out to the Coast to try to escape myself. I moved to Los Angeles, got a job in burlesque and met a girl I liked very much. Her name was Grace Hathaway, same name as Shakespeare's girl friend. I married her. It was no more than a year after the first marriage had ended. I wondered at the time what had happened. I was really establishing the same pattern. In other words, the pattern in my consciousness hadn't worked out.

But the second time, there wasn't that sentimentality with the children. I didn't feel that I had to have them with me and possess them, although I loved them very much. It was as if I was friends with the kids. We were friends. So the relationship was quite different than with my first kids. Then I hated it like hell when a person was gone 'cause it was like tearing away a part of me.

I never heard anything from my first two kids. But there is no sadsackness about it. No "Oh, I long to see them, I've got to return . . . ." None of that. I was part of their coming through and that's that. But when I was with them and they were taken away from me, it was awful. Now I admit she only had three or four affairs and I had three dozen, but it didn't matter. You know, "This is mine, mine."

What happened with Gracie is that I was too slow for her. She was working at Eddie Spolak's joint and I was working at "Goman's Gay Nineties." We had three kids and we were living in Vallejo. I was doing all the work with the kids, getting their meals and all that, because I had to work at night. The little girl was about seven or eight. The oldest boy, the adopted one was about fourteen. My son was around twelve. By this time I had more or less settled down. What I always did, before I married Guin, was almost incestuous in terms of the age difference between me and the women.

Now the third one, she was an executive secretary. Her mind was strictly on money. So she picked the wrong one when she picked me. There was about fifteen years difference between us. It didn't last long.

So how does this all work out to me being who I am now? Well, there's that verse at the front end of *Light on the Path,* "**Before the eyes can see, they must be incapable of tears . . . .**" Because they understand that they were never born and will never die and they have only to show empathy and love for everyone. "**Before the ears can hear, they must have lost their sensitiveness . . . .**" So that anything said against you, regardless of who said it or how lousy it is, it don't break you up and you don't lose your cool. "**Before the voice can speak in the Presence of the Masters, it must have lost its power to wound . . . .**" So what you say to them, regardless of what they do to you, is kind whether they are aware of it or not. "**Before the feet can stand in the Presence of the Masters, they must be washed in the blood of the heart . . . .**" So that your very understanding will have become of that HEART'S BLOOD, the ESSENCE of LIFE ITSELF that is kept alive by the breath and the INFINITE POWER that is flowing through us all.

Then there's something else that Mabel Collins wrote in another book:

> There are three truths which are absolute and which cannot be lost, but which may remain silent from the lack of speech.
>
> The soul of Man is immortal, and its future is the future of a thing whose growth and splendor have no limit.
>
> The principle which gives us life dwells in us, without us, is undying and eternally beneficent. It is not heard or seen or smelt, but is perceived by the man who desires perception.
>
> Each man is his own absolute law-giver, the dispenser of glory or gloom to himself, and the decreer of his life, his reward, and his punishment.
>
> These truths which are as great as life itself are as simple as the simplest mind of man. Feed the hungry with them.
>
> *Idyll of The White Lotus,* p. 123.

Words we manufacture in our heads. But what's behind the words bleeds through to whoever's listening. You each carry the chalice within your own heart, what you give is up to you, what you withhold is up to you. You can make it narrow or confining, or grasping or you can let it be a gesture of compassion to everybody. It's not a profitable way to live. You don't end up with a fortune or anything like that. But believe me, if you follow the laws that are stated in those three truths, you'll always be taken care of.

You're There Now, Stay There!

I'm going to tell you a little bit about Dr. W.Y. Evans-Wentz [25], about my meeting with him, because this has a bearing on what I want to show you. The story starts right here in the S.F. lodge. When I moved to this part of the country, I started coming to the meetings here. The lodge librarian was a woman named Agnes Kast. If you came in and asked Agnes for a book from the library, she wouldn't ask you what author or title you wanted, she would just walk over to one of the book cases and get a book out and hand it to you. The happy part of it was that nine times out of ten, she'd hand you a book that would fit with what you were looking for. Well, she swore up and down that she wasn't psychic or any of that stuff, but that's the way it would turn out.

I told her some of the things I was interested in and she handed me *The Tibetan Book of the Dead*, then I read *Tibet's Great Yogi, Milarepa*, both authored by Dr. Evans-Wentz. Next, I read his *Tibetan Yoga and Secret Doctrine*, which he thought would be the last book he would write.

Afterwards, however, he took another trip back to India and the Himalayas and found someone who introduced him to a manuscript which formed the basis of the *The Tibetan Book of the Great Liberation*, and turned out to be the last one he put out. When it came finally out, I put it together with everything else I had been studying.

In fact, up to that point, and through that time, I thought that using the love element as the important thing was sloppy, like "Wow, it can't be there, in the heart, it's gotta be here, in the head." But this thing, the heart, kept bugging me all the time, it kept on coming all the time . . . .

While I was studying Evans-Wentz, I still didn't know anything about ZEN. So when I had my belly full of Evans-Wentz, I wanted to know what ZEN was all about, so I looked into that. And all of a sudden, everything started to open up. You could see the connection between all of it. At first, these had been separate things. But then when I looked again, wow!

It starts to open up inside, and you start getting a better understanding of the Whole. No psychic gimmicks, none of that. Just seeing it all, it's clear to you, you see it.

With Evans-Wentz, it all fit. Not so much in reading *Book of the Dead*, although that answered some questions. But in the other one, *Yoga and Secret Doctrine*, I got into it very much. There was this thing called the *Doctrine of The Clear Light*. And CLEAR LIGHT, you can't even see. So I read that one on the Clear Light, then I got through to *Yoga of The Long Hum*. There all the colors were synthesized in the Vajra-Sattva thing, it's a very short deal.

In the *Long Hum*, it says, "MAY THE VAJRA OF THE HEART BE REALIZED IN THIS LIFETIME." And do you know what VAJRA means in Tibetan? Heart, the diamond of the heart. And the diamond, when it's polished, can reflect any facet or color in existence. And it's the hardest gem. We even use it to make drills that bore down through rock. Yet it can accommodate everything that comes. So when you're having a tough time and life is giving you hell, then you know the Divine Lapidary is just polishing another jewel of consciousness. That's not a bad line, is it?

So I read his books. Then I thought I'd like to write a letter to this guy and meet him. Well, the only place I could think of to write him was the Oxford University Press in England. At that time, there was no paperback out. So I wrote him a letter. Three months went by, and I didn't get any answer. So I thought, "Oh well, he's a bigshot, or he took off or whatever, you know, don't worry about it."

Finally, I get a letter from him. I found out he owns a hotel in San Diego, the Keystone. What a name, it reminded me of the Keystone Cops. It was a real dinky place. He said that he had just gotten my letter. It had gone to London, then back to New York, then New York forwarded it to him. And they weren't in a hurry about it. He said, "I'd like to have you come down and see me."

WOW, it's a big deal! All this has been my hobby for years, studying everything of this nature. WOW! So that's the one side, the other side was making a living. At that time, I was working in a barbershop quartet—making people laugh, making people cry and hoping that on the overtone there would be some help going out to them, so that they'd come loose a little.

So I got a ticket. I had to leave after the last show. I had to get out a little early to get to the airport and catch the last flight. I only had one day a week off. When he met me in San Diego, he wanted to walk into the airplane to inspect it. That shows how weird he was. In all his world-traveling, he had never journeyed on an airplane.

I looked at this guy. After all, I was talking to someone high on the hog. I didn't know how I'd be received. Me, with my eigth grade education. So he took me to his hotel. He asked which of his books I liked best. Now remember, at that time *The Great Liberation* hadn't been published yet, so I said I liked *Tibetan Yoga and Secret Doctrine* the best. He asked which part of it I liked best. I said I liked *Clear Light* and the *Six Jewels of Tilopa* best. He said that there was a book coming out that would be the answer for what I wanted to know. That's all he put out. Does he tell me the name of the book? No.

He said the only other person that made a special trip to talk to him was Theo Bernard. "But," he said, "I'm not too happy with him because he published a couple of things that are misquotes."

So I had to wait for this book to come out, *The Great Liberation*. This is the book that's supposed to do it for me. It was about 1959. When it came out, I started reading it, and I read it every morning for six months. I read it over and over again. It didn't seem like there was anything there, although I was expecting to get something out of it. But anyway, I didn't get anything.

So, at the end of the six months, I called a lady we knew from L.A., a very psychic baroness. She said, "When I'm talking to you, I see a mediterranean blue sky." That's great, but it doesn't help any. So, I thought, "Well, I'll just keep on reading it." I'm a stubborn Capricorn.

Then one morning, I hear a voice saying, "TRANSPARENT JEWEL, TRANSPARENT JEWEL . . . ." I thought, "At last, you've flipped out, you've popped your cork." "*TRANSPARENT JEWEL, TRANSPARENT JEWEL . . . .*"

And I thought, "I've heard that name before." Then I remembered Mabel Collins had written a book called *The Transparent Jewel*, a translation of *The Yoga Sutras of Patanjali*. She said that you should make your mind like a clear magnifying glass, so you could get other thoughts out of it. Then whatever the subject was, you could lay it all out and see it clearly.

Then the sky started to fall in on me, I realized that I was being told, very abruptly and succinctly, exactly how to get this part, the head, entirely and completely clear, so that I could dig the other part, the heart.

All right, it meant something to me, and yet it didn't. How could I apply it? So I can put all my attention on one thing, concentration. I can not only think of a thing with all my attention, I can make it *samyana*, that is, collecting all the faculties into the one-pointedness, and in contemplation, it'll spread out again and contract.

I had started reading the footnotes in *The Great Liberation* by this time, and I read about Ramana Maharshi. So I get through with this job at Goman's, and I get a job in a movie house, taking tickets, with the glorious title of "night manager," which means you're just a stooge around the joint. While I'm there, I would go down around the corner to Holmes Bookstore on my lunch hour, to look at the second-hand books. In there, I run across three of Ramana Maharshi's little books in the second-hand occult section. I think it cost me a grand total of sixty-three cents. I took 'em home and read 'em and said to myself, "WOW! This makes the whole *Great Liberation* and the rest of it just ZUNK!" It all comes like that from reading this thing. I see a little more how to apply it. This was my introduction to Ramana Maharshi.

By this time, as far as color and music was concerned, I had realized all the color comes from the breaking up of the Clear Light itself, so therefore there is a point of synthesis prior to the fact of any color's particular angle. Therefore, it must be the same way with the mind. The way it sees things is color.

Next, I met Guin. Guin, right away, with her sharp mind dug it through *The Diamond Sutra*. She handed me *The Diamond Sutra* and I read it and said, "Okay." But for me, it didn't do it. But the *Six Rules of Tilopa*, she agreed, had it. So just as she has so kindly put music to the words we found in various scriptures, she wrote music for the *Six Rules of Tilopa*. So I figured, "Well, I would like Evans-Wentz to hear this."

We called up the hotel, he was there. We got through to his room and his nurse put him on the phone. I said, "This is Joe Miller." He said, "Are you downstairs..?" I said, "No, I'm in San Francisco, my wife, Guin, has written some music, and I would like to have you hear it." So she played it and I sang it into the phone. Evans-Wentz' voice had been very weak and feeble, but after listening to the song, he shouted "YOU'RE THERE

NOW, STAY THERE!" That was my okay from him that I had dug what it was all about. I didn't know whether it was Guin's music or my pushiness that put it over. We corresponded with him, and he gave us permission to use any quotes from his books.

When he said that to me, "YOU'RE THERE NOW, STAY THERE," it did something INSIDE of me. But it didn't do something to my head or to the so-called "kundalini," it did something to the HEART!

Joe holding forth   *Joe holding back*

The center cannot hold. The child knows something.

Joe, the student prince. Early 1920s. Here he and friends illustrate how attached we get to our various roles.

Early 1930s, the doe-eyed gangster

PART THREE:

Great Liberation

Editor's Note

In this section, you'll find Joe's commentary on *The Great Liberation* along with excerpts from the sutra itself. The indented text is from *The Great Liberation*. Everything flush with the lefthand margin is Joe's commentary. The titles, "Salutations to the One Mind," "The Yoga of the Thatness," etc., are taken, as is the text of the sutra, from the Oxford University Press edition of *The Tibetan Book of The Great Liberation*, which also includes introductory materials by Dr. Evans-Wentz and Carl Jung, a biography of Padma Sambhava, and extensive footnotes.

The "Precious Guru," Padma Sambhava, traveled from Kashmir to Tibet in the late 8th Century and established the high *dharma* teachings there. *The Tibetan Book of The Great Liberation* stands as his ultimate expression. It is "the yoga of knowing the mind in its nakedness," and extols what Dr. Carl Jung, in his introduction, called "the self-liberating power of the introverted mind."

The original text of *The Great Liberation* was written down by Padma Sambhava's foremost disciple and consort, the Lady Yeshe Tsogyal, "who served the Nirmanakaya Orgyen Padma from her eighth year, accompanying him as a shadow follows a body." Tsogyal hid *The Great Liberation* along with many other writings, ritual objects, and relics in the deep caves and pools of the Himalayas. Discovered centuries later, these scrolls and other objects were able to provide certain essential teachings in a pure and undiluted form.

Joe often mentioned that some "authorities," including Lama Govinda, were upset with Dr. Evans-Wentz for publishing this particular text. "They considered it very secret and esoteric," Joe explained, "for only those who had gone through a lot of other stuff first." But Evans-Wentz wanted to get the teachings out and into the hands of *everyman*. And Joe, with the Tea Party blood of his forefathers, took it a wild step or two further. Every lenten season, Joe would rise at 6:30 A.M. to read the sutra out loud to whoever considered it important enough to struggle up Nob Hill in the chill, pre-dawn darkness.

Joe's approach to the presentation of these teachings was rather unorthodox. One of the more traditional ways to approach the teachings of

Padma Sambhava and the Lady Yeshe Tsogyal is through the preliminaries of *guru yoga*. H.H. Dilgo Khyentse Rinpoche, meditation master to the Dalai Lama, wrote of this yoga in *The Wish-Fulfilling Gem* and *The Excellent Path To Enlightenment*. Traditionally, visualizations are utilized. For example, Padma Sambhava is seen with three severed head dangling from his trident—a freshly severed one to symbolize the future, a decaying one to symbolize the present and a dried skull to symbolize the past. Yeshe Tsogyal is seen as *Vajra Yogini*—with a brilliant, translucent red body, and her lips slightly parted to reveal sharp teeth. She is holding a curved sword to cut through the ego and its poisons, and a cup of *amrita*, the nectar of deathlessness. The beautiful seven-branched prayer with its prostrations, confession, and offerings and other elements common to the various guru yogas of Tibet are also incorporated.

Joe wasn't against this kind of practice. He simply had other work to do. He wanted to launch a few key notions into people's consciousnesses, like "AS A THING IS VIEWED, SO IT APPEARS," or "THE SEEING OF THE RADIANCE OF THIS WISDOM (OR MIND) WHICH SHINES WITHOUT BEING PERCEIVED IS BUDDHAHOOD," in the hope that these notions get chewed on and mulled over and lived with for awhile, so that they could lead the seeker to a perpetually deepening view of the world and the self.

Some Remarks on *The Great Liberation*

The Great Liberation is something that you individually find out and work with yourself. Not by going without, but by going within. Yes, we have a library, a wonderful library. But, you see, we weren't born with a book for a head. Nor do we die with a book for a head. It's all right to have book-learning in the beginning so that you understand what it's all about, but you have to find that reality within yourselves.

If you find it just within your head, by a process of reasoning and intellectual faculties, I'm afraid it would be pretty dry. Of course, it's necessary to use those faculties, but the intelligence factor of the higher mind as presented by Theosophy resides in the heart of each individual. Not on the left-hand side or the right-hand side, but in the middle. That's what each one of us have to get to.

Normally, we don't get very close to it. Because we have some particular situation or combination that's happening in our personal lives that binds us to that situation of our own, instead of getting free from that and finding that feeling of the very ONENESS underneath it all that comes from the Heart. We don't get to it.

Now *The Great Liberation* is a method of realizing NIRVANA through knowing the mind.

Most of us have something that we've tucked away back in our consciousness that we don't wish to look at. Maybe it was an event or action in our early youth that has left a mark that we are continually reacting to, without looking at it and saying, "Where did this come from?" In fact, a number of years ago, it would have been considered a great crime if you questioned your own consciousness and common sense as they called it.

But common sense is a very rare commodity. Only a few people have common sense. Because the use of the word *common* would mean that it would be all-inclusive and few people want to feel that everybody has as much as they've got. They want it to be a private institution and they say, "I'm going to do this for me and nobody else can do it!" We've had dictators that tried that too. They decided they were going to have everybody think the same way and do just what they told them to.

The Great Liberation is of Buddhist inspiration. And Buddha said, even as Christ would have if he had been asked, "I am an ordinary man. I have found this out by inquiring into it. I have found out that with my consciousness I can get to a place where I am at one and yet (I'm ad-libbing again, this last part) I can still be an individual and always will be an individual."

And so will each one of you always be individuals. You know it's rather silly that you should even be here. It's a beautiful night, the weather's good. You could be down on the beach or sitting at home looking at the boob tube until your eyes got as big as musk melons. But you all must have had some experience somewhere else that tells you that there is a way and that you did touch it. And know as even the Master Jesus said, YOU individually are "the way, the truth, and the life." The life that's within you is in everything.

The time is coming when it will be necessary for enough of you to have fallen awake, that when the other people are lost and don't know where to turn, they can come to you directly with a question on it and you can help them. You can tell them that it is within themselves that they will find the answer. No one can give it to you. They can tell you about it. But the EXPERIENCE must be yours, and if you don't have the experience, you haven't got it.

Of course, you might reply, "That's all right to say, but when do we get the experience?" You all have had some of the experiences already. And, in fact, every night when you go to sleep, you go through a routine that takes you to a place of DEEP SLEEP. When you're in deep sleep, that part of your being is AT HOME with the Reality.

The Great Liberation teaches how to work your way through it from the mind to THE MIND. Look at it clearly. We have our conscious mind working outwardly, our objective mind, and we have our subjective mind with all the thoughts we think in our heads (that's where we keep our darkest ones).

If I could just take you out of your heads for a moment or so all of this stuff that you are working on and worrying about ("How am I going to get this? What should I do with that? Where will we go from here? Is my work going to stand up or am I going to be out on my butt in the cold and sleeping in the park?"), you would see that underneath it all is that SUBSTRATUM of REALITY that is giving you life.

How much do you think we are all effected by the ads we see on the boob-tube? You keep hearing the same thing over and over and over again, then you go somewhere and you want something cold to drink and you say, "Oh, make it Coca-Cola."

We are all victims of our desires and our experiences. That's why we're in these particular incarnations. Because something wasn't completed at another time. Possibly some of the last things we thought of (Oh, if I could have only have had that!). So you come back in with that drive, "I gotta have that!" Then, you have the commercials to make sure that you keep having drives. If all commercials were cut off immediately and there were no ads in the paper or on the radio, business would be shot to hell. It would just take a few days and it would slow it all up. But that's all right for this level we're on here.

Because this level that we're on here is just as spiritual as any far off, imaginary place where they float around with beautiful balloons in their eyeballs. This hunk of table, everything in the joint, is just as spiritual as I am! It's all part of the very ONENESS, and you're part of that very ONENESS and you have to come to it sooner or later. If you don't do it this time, you'll have to do it some other time.

I'm trying to crack your heads together so that you will realize that you can have it this time! This time! If you can just be still, VERY STILL, so still that the thoughts aren't running around in your head. If you had cockroaches in the house, you'd spray 'em wouldn't ya? Why don't you do the same thing with the thoughts in your head, then realize that in the STILLNESS, you're AT ONE with the very REALITY. [26]

I'll tell you a little trick I played on the kids who came to listen to *The Great Liberation.* Each morning, when we got through with the reading, I hit the gong, and I would say, "Now listen with concentration on the tone of that gong." And when the gong stopped, just in that second—you were there, you were right on that place. Because you weren't thinking any thoughts in the lower mind, and you were aware of the reality that you were aware.

If you met somebody who had never tasted honey, how would you explain the taste to them? You couldn't do it. They have to experience it. And the *peace that passeth understanding* that's in your hearts and minds, I can't explain that either. You have to experience it.

It can't be taught, it has to be caught.

What the hell are you doing here? You came because some guy's talking about *The Great Liberation.* **THE GREAT LIBERATION IS WITHIN YOU AND YOU ARE LIBERATED NOW!** Except that your lower mind is saying, "Oh well, I could give up this, but I couldn't give up that." You can't look at it impersonally. "Oh, there's gotta be that attachment that I feel." **Come on, dig it, dig it, dig it!**

If just one person gets a touch of something during this period that we are here together, it was more than worthwhile for you all to be here. Because it is all a Oneness. Each one of us IS that Reality, in Essence.

And a *PARTICULAR* part of that reality. I'll prove it to you. Show me any two people with the same finger-prints. If that individual identity is here on this plane, I'm sure it continues at all levels. Each of you has a part to play in it.

I'll tell you a story.

I was working in a burlesque house (a very cultured place to be workin', eh?). I would come home at two o'clock in the morning and go up on the roof of the apartment house. Probably wait there 'till sunrise. If I did a midnight show and didn't get home until after three o'clock, I didn't have long to wait.

And as the sun was coming up, all my friends, the little birds would start singing MADLY, throwing themselves into it and singing. That's one of the reasons I can't eat birds, chicken or turkey. Because they told me something. Those birds were saying that each day in life we go into deep sleep and come out of it in the morning, just as the planet moves around, and catch the rays from that source from which we receive our greatest energy, the sun.

They FELT it. They were singing the sun up. They weren't only singing that, they were singing because in their hearts they were a conscious part of it in their own way, in their own form of consciousness. They'll find out how tough it is when they get in these human physical bodies later on.

Come on, you got all these beautiful things. This isn't something somebody else can give you. You gotta find it. You already got it. Just BE it.

So you say, "Well, you've been talking about this *just being* it for a long time, Miller, but I think you're a little nuts." Understood. But I'm also happy and CONTENTED and contentment is the real wealth. I'm doing my own thing. And my thing is to just keep telling my story and while I'm telling, I just keep radiating love out to all of you.

Excerpts from *The Great Liberation* with Joe's Commentary

SALUTATIONS TO THE ONE MIND

All hail to the One Mind that embraces the whole sangsara and nirvana, That eternally is as it is, yet is unknown, That, although ever clear and ever existing, is not visible, That, although radiant and unobscured, is not recognized.

To the great consciousness of which we are all just individual parts with our own particular character and possibilities. Remember that throughout this sutra, the one mind represents consciousness, not the brain of anyone, but THE consciousness!

THE RESULT OF NOT KNOWING THE ONE MIND

Knowledge of that which is vulgarly called mind is wide-spread.
Inasmuch as the One Mind is unknown, or thought of erroneously, or known one-sidedly without being thoroughly known as it is, desire for these teachings will be immeasurable.
They will also be sought after by ordinary individuals, who, not knowing the One Mind, do not know themselves.
They wander hither and thither in the three regions, and thus among the six classes of beings, suffering sorrow.
Such is the result of their error of not having attained understanding of their mind.
Because their suffering is in every way overpowering, even self-control is lacking to them.
Thus, although one may wish to know the mind as it is, one fails.

The brain is the tool that the mind, or consciousness, uses and we are individual divisions of that One Consciousness. But we must reach through to the One Consciousness and we have a center within ourselves which we can reach to and find. It's all within each one of us. This is to explain how you might get there. It goes so slowly and it repeats things all through it. It is for each one that is here to take in their own way and look at from their own view-point. If you find it worthwhile, use it. If you don't, forget about it!

The Result of Desires

> Others, in accordance with their own particular faith and practice, having become fettered by desires, cannot perceive the Clear Light.

"Fettered" meaning fastened to, but if you can escape from the desires, if you can enjoy them and not let them enjoy you, everything goes along all right. In non-attachment, you can enjoy the desires as long as you know that you are always above, beyond, and through them all. It's speaking here of desire for possession, rather than aspiration toward the reality. You can enjoy everything in life that comes to you, but don't try to possess it privately.

> They are overwhelmed by suffering, and are in darkness because of their suffering.

After all, if you desire and want to possess something, you can only hold it as long as you're in incarnation anyhow. Desires never live up to their promises. After you get the thing that you say, "Well, if I got it, the world would be entirely different. I wouldn't want anything else," it usually takes a few days for you to start reaching for something else, rather than finding out who you really are within you, and enjoying and accepting what comes to you. But you kiss it on the fly and it's gone. **If you could retain that spark of the spirituality that's in that first part of "falling in love" and stay in that place, you've already graduated out of the lower aspects and you're living in the higher mind.**

MIND IN ITS TRUE STATE

> When one seeks one's mind in its true state, it is found to be quite
> intelligible, although invisible.
> In its true state, mind is naked, immaculate; not made of anything,
> being of the voidness; clear, vacuous, without duality,
> transparent; timeless, uncompounded, unimpeded, colourless;
> not realizable as a separate thing, but as the unity of all things,
> yet not composed of them; of one taste, and transcendent over
> differentiation.
> Nor is one's mind separable from other minds.

Now "mind in its true state," that doesn't mean mind in any special person,
but consciousness in anyone and everyone, its pure essence and its true
state. That means the stuff of awareness that you use in your own head
right now, your common ordinary mind! This is a part of that greater
consciousness. But you're obscuring the particular part of it that fits in
with your own particular soap opera that you're running. This section is
describing the state of consciousness if you can get to it and enjoy it and
realize it as it actually is for each and every one of us. This is that facet
of consciousness that is contained in that Point within you, and what you
each individually ARE in that Clearness.

There's that state where it's all one if you can just clear it like a looking
glass. Just see the stuff go by and be aware of it. Or like old man Milarepa
sitting by the side of the river watching the stuff go by. You don't have
to pick up everything that goes by in the stream. In fact, with as much
pollution as there is in the city, it could be embarrassing. Just let it go by.
WATCH IT! Watch it. Be aware of it.

> To realize the quintessential being of the One Mind is to realize the
> immutable at-one-ment of the tri-kaya.

The Tibetans refer to the three-fold expression of the Oneness as the
tri-kaya, as in Christianity we refer to the Father, Son, and Holy Ghost.
Remember, each great religion shows the path to that reality. But we—in
the western world—must have the freedom of consciousness also. Otherwise, we're lost, or we're dopes and get pushed around. But if we have
that and the heart in union . . . .Well, it's like those pictures you see of the
Dhyana Buddhas in their association with the opposite sex, the figures in
coition are the heart and mind conjoined.

The mind, being, as the uncreated and of the voidness, the dharma-kaya, and, as the vacuous and self-radiant, the sambhoga-kaya, and, as the unobscured, shining for all living creatures, the nirmana-kaya, is the primordial essence wherein its three divine aspects are one.

These three are One, it's just divided so that within your consciousness you can understand that it is all contained in the very Oneness itself. Dharma-kaya being clear light. Sambhoga-kaya being all the things that you can imagine, that which allows you to run your own movies and build your own software in your head. The nirmana-kaya is realizing the Oneness of it all, realizing that in essence actually this manifestation that we are functioning in at the present time is unity itself in diversity, our diversified expressions, each one an original because each is a part of the Oneness itself.

Now the three divine aspects are the universal tri-kaya. It's there too but it's in each one of us individually. We have the dharma-kaya, the sambhoga-kaya, and the nirmana-kaya all within each one of us. Those three divisions are explaining its utility. **Now think of it for a moment and realize that we are microcosmic reflections of the macrocosm, the solar system. So we have the three within us. The dharma-kaya is the Clear Light. The sambhoga-kaya is all the fantasies that you want to build, the beautiful dreams that you can see, what we do with our imaginations. We can build up a horrible or lovely world. We each have our own soap operas and we're living in a bigger soap opera.** It's the effect of all humanity going through the various phases of learning that are necessary for it to come to a higher point in its evolution.

In other words, each of us is a portion of that primordial divine essence, but within that we have these capacities—that of seeing it clearly—dharmakaya—that of making any kind of fantasy we want and making it self-radiant—sambhogakaya—and then that of love for every-one, the primordial essence—nirmana-kaya.

Mind is Non-Created

Mind in its true nature being non-created and self-radiant, how can one, without knowing the mind, assert that mind is created?

After the body is dropped, Mind is still there.

> There being in this yoga nothing objective upon which to meditate, how can one, without having ascertained the true nature of meditation, assert that mind is created?

> Mind in its true state being reality, how can one, without having discovered one's own mind, assert that mind is created?

So you meditate and get to the place of samadhi and you realize you've gotten clear, what do you do with it? Are you gonna use the other two parts of the tri-kaya or are you just gonna say, "Well, I've had it clear for awhile, now I wanna go back to sleep and re-learn all these things I've got on record?"

> Mind in its true state being undoubtedly ever-existing, how can one, without having seen the mind face to face, assert that mind is created?

When you try to "see the mind face to face," you don't see a face, you come to awareness and you're still alive and can observe but the mind itself is not in one hunk floating around somewhere. You don't see IT, you BE IT, you FEEL IT. You can't see IT because IT is No-Thing, IT is in a higher dimension and yet that higher dimension is functioning in part through you, with things fastened onto it and holding you back from understanding it because of your individual hang-ups.

> The thinking-principle being of the very essence of mind, how can one, without having sought and found it, assert that mind is created?

> Mind being transcendent over creation, and thus partaking of the Uncreated, how can one assert that mind is created?

Mind is "transcendent over creation and thus partaking of the uncreated," and yet nevertheless the creative as well is all part of the very Oneness. There is no duality. It's one reality. That's why we have to learn to live here and understand there, before we can live here and have understanding here by falling awake.

> Being in its primordial, unmodified naturalness non-created, as it should be taken to be, and without form, how can one assert that it is created?

As Tilopa said, "Keep in the Natural State," a state of awareness of everything that is going on and say, "It's a movie. I'm watching it. It's my own movie plus the movies everyone else is putting on."

> Inasmuch as mind can also be taken to be devoid of quality, how can one venture to assert that it is created?

> The self-born, qualityless mind, being like the three voids undifferentiated, unmodified, how can one assert that mind is created?

It's part of the very Oneness. It's all a Oneness. Not some high-class place that you have to get into by tying yourself into a knot or beating yourself to death. Our ordinary mind is sustained and maintained by that very Oneness itself.

> Mind being without objectivity and causation, self-originated, self-born, how can one, without having endeavored to know mind, assert that mind is created?

> Inasmuch as divine wisdom dawns in accordance with its own time, and one is emancipated, how can opponents of these teachings assert that it is created?

In other words, by the expansion of your own consciousness, the growth in your particular understanding of what life is all about. This comes from within by that spark of infinity within you. When you are ripe for it. You can't make it happen! You can't do anything to bring it about forcefully. You'd only be getting a lousy imitation of what the reality is. We just have to keep on going and expanding with it. You come to the place where it happens. It happens with spontaneity, and you say, "Now I knew that all the time, but I didn't have it where I could handle it in my own individual expression." In your own time, when you ripen ever as flowers are ripe, you'll burst into blossom. You've come here to find out about the essence of it!

Do you realize one of the lamas, Lama Govinda, said that the particular sutra we're reading shouldn't be given to common people because they wouldn't understand it. It would just lead them astray. "Let 'em bow on their knees and butt their heads on the floor and kiss it. You know what I mean? Go on and on for a thousand times or two or three years and well, now we'll tell you all about it." I say, WHY NOT TELL 'EM ABOUT IT NOW!

> Mind being, as it is, of this nature, and thus unknowable, how can
> one assert that it is created?

It isn't created. It's eternal! It's consciousness itself. "Consciousness without an object is." Your consciousness can be without an object of attention and you can still be aware of it. You can run it the way you want to instead of it running you.

THE GREAT LIGHT

> This yoga also concerns the foundation of the immutable great
> light.
> The teaching of this changeless great light is of the unique clear
> wisdom here set forth, which, illuminating the three times, is
> called the light.
> The meditation upon this changeless great light is of the unique
> clear wisdom here set forth, which, illuminating the three
> times, is called the light.
> The practice relating to this changeless great light is of the unique
> clear wisdom here set forth, which illuminating the three
> times, is called the light.

This is the light that's not seen on land or sea, the light that lives within you and me, the light that makes it all function. You see with your eyes but you never see light. All you see is the reflection and refraction thereof, but it is, just the same as breathing just is.

THE DOCTRINE OF THE THREE TIMES

> The essence of the doctrine concerning the three times in at-one-
> ment will now be expounded.
> The yoga concerning the past and future not being practiced,
> memory of the past remains latent. The future, not being
> welcomed, is completely severed by the mind from the present.
> The present, not being fixable, remains in the state of the voidness.

Or, in other words, in the looking glass. You're just watching it go on, being aware of it. Voidness, Clear Light! The present is a moving line. Everything is action in this universe. When they say "BE STILL," and you see some great teacher being still, just remember there's more whirling going on there than you could ever imagine and that's what's affecting you and making you be there. You're digging a little something without thinking about it. Voidness does not mean a blackness. The mind itself is an awareness.

The Yoga of the Nirvanic Path

> There being no thing upon which to meditate, no meditation is
> there whatsoever.

Because if you're meditating, you're meditating on an idea and that's a concept. Therefore, you're staying in the brain content instead of getting clear from it and getting deep into the heart where the reality lives.

> There being no thing to go astray, no going astray is there, if one be
> guided by memory.
> Without meditating, without going astray, look into the True State,
> wherein self-cognition, self-knowledge, self-illumination
> shine resplendently. These, so shining, are called "The
> Bodhisattvic Mind."
> In the realm of wisdom, transcendent overall meditation, naturally
> illuminative, where there is no going astray, the vacuous
> concepts, the self-liberation, and the primordial voidness are
> of the dharma-kaya.

Just looking at it clearly, not being hung-up on anything.

> Without realization of this, the goal of the nirvanic path is
> unattainable.
> Simultaneously with its realization the vajra-sattva state is realized.

The vajra-sattva state is the state we're all trying for whether we know it or not. Vajra means diamond, it also means heart. *Sattva* means perfect harmony, the eternal harmony, harmony of the heart. So, the "vajra-sattva state" means the marriage of the heart and the head within you.

> These teachings are exhaustive of all knowledge, exceedingly deep,

and immeasurable.

> Although, they are to be contemplated in a variety of ways, to this
> Mind of self-cognition and self-originated wisdom, there are
> no two such things as contemplation and contemplator.

You see this is carrying you to a different level of consciousness, a level of consciousness where there is pure mind, pure reality, pure consciousness. If your personality were interfering you'd be working with the limitations of your lower mind, but if the contemplation and contemplator were not there, you'd be into the Clear State.

> When exhaustively contemplated, these teachings merge in at-one-
> ment with the scholarly seeker who has sought them, although
> the seeker himself when sought cannot be found.

You say, "How does this happen? This is all right, if you're talking about someone else but what the hell has this got to do with me?" I'll tell you what it's got to do with you. When you get hung-up on something—I don't care whether it's hay or nose-candy, a man, a woman, something that you have to have, an extra car or whatever the hell it is—you're not thinking anything, you're not living anything. At that moment, you're being the car, you're being the other person, you're GONE. So why can't you be GONE in an understanding of the reality? Just whap! Huh? Did you ever get hooked on anything? Complete desire? You just had to have it? When you get hooked enough, you can't think of anything else? You're no longer there. So if you realize that you're living from the Oneness, you're letting God, the reality live through you. You wouldn't be there but everything you have in your personality would be used to carry that on. In other words, as a guy writes, GOD SEND ME, I'M READY! Try it sometime. It'll scare the hell out of you what comes out of it.

> Thereupon is attained the goal of the seeking, and also the end of
> the search itself. Then, nothing more is there to be sought; nor
> is there need to seek anything.
> This beginningless, vacuous, unconfused clear wisdom of self-
> cognition is the very same as that set forth in the doctrine of
> the Great Perfection.

The doctrine of the great perfection is love. Love is *bhakti*. Pure love—the all-inclusive, the great compassion that includes everything. That's the way of the *Great Perfection*. This *Great Liberation* is the *jnani* way, the thinking way, the logical way, for you to get to the place where you drop the logic and you're into the Oneness itself. The *Great Perfection* is that of the heart. When you divide up that tri-kaya that you heard about earlier, it's the nirmanakaya part that wants to help everybody fall awake. So that they can feel themselves at one with the very Oneness, that pure unbiased universal love and compassion is the way of the *Great Perfection*. The doctrine of the *Great Perfection* is coming to the realization and the ecstasy which takes you beyond the human kingdom and graduates you from this kindergarten on this little off-beat planet called Earth, it's really quite different, so they tell me. Pure love is not possessive, it's a giving, an understanding there are only two kinds of people in the world really, givers and takers. The predominant one seems to be takers, givers are rather a rare commodity. But if we learn about that it doesn't mean we give the shoes off our feet or the coats off our backs. But radiate that love to everybody and know that it is universal.

> Although there are no two such things as knowing and not know-
> ing, there are profound and innumerable sorts of meditation;
> and surpassingly excellent it is in the end to know one's mind.

Sure, to know all the places that contemplation can sneak into and say, "Oh yes, this is the biggest thing, this is the most important thing." THE THING IS TO BE TURNED LOOSE! PLOW IT UNDER and THEN CULTIVATE THE WHOLE THING and LOOK AT IT AS AWARENESS, huh? This don't mean you forget anything you've done or been or seen. But you don't let it affect you. Yesterday is gone, tomorrow ain't here yet. Now is the time!

> There being no two such things as object of meditation and
> meditator, if by those who practice or do not practice
> meditation, the meditator of the meditation be sought and
> not found; thereupon the goal of the meditation is reached and
> also the end of the meditation itself.
> There being no two such things as meditation and object of
> meditation, there is no need to fall under the sway of deeply
> obscuring ignorance; for, as the result of meditation upon
> the unmodified quiescence of mind, the non-created wisdom
> instantaneously shines forth clearly.

I'll read that last again because it's telling you something, if you want to try it, "For as a result of meditation upon the unmodified quiescence of mind, the non-created wisdom instantaneously shines forth clearly."

> Although there is an innumerable variety of profound practices, to
> one's mind in its true state they are non-existent; for there are
> no two such things as existence and non-existence.

It's all part of consciousness. It's all a slide show or a movie or a TV. When
we find out that we're the one handling the machine and all the stations
belong to us, we can adjust any one of 'em we wanna. When we decide
to drop our own private soap opera in our own minds for a little while we
find the sun is shining and it's a beautiful day.

> There being no two such things as practice and practitioner, if
> by those who practice or do not practice the practitioner of
> practice be sought and not found, thereupon the goal of the
> practice is reached and also the end of the practice itself.
> Inasmuch as from eternity, there is nothing whatsoever to be
> practiced, there is no need to fall under the sway of errant
> propensities.

No, don't fall under the sway of errant propensities. Why not? You've got
nothing to lose. It's always up to you. No one else can do it for you. No
one can dunk you in a bucket of water and say, "You've got it!" You can
just sit tied up like a pretzel or observe your belly till it gets as big as a
wash-tub. That's got nothing to do with it. You've got to find IT in your
own consciousness.

> The non-created, self-radiant wisdom here set forth, being action-
> less, immaculate, transcendent over acceptance or rejection, is
> itself the perfect practice.

So we're doing a practice all the time, but we're not doing the practice in
its BIG way really. We're only practicing to keep the things alive in our
own cotton-pickin' minds!

> Although there are no two such things as pure and impure, there
> is an innumerable variety of fruits of yoga, all of which, to
> one's mind in its true state, are the conscious content of the
> non-created tri-kaya.

Sure, you built it yourself. It's the parts that went by that you liked, that
you stuck in there and that you're using in your own set-up.

> There being no two such things as action and performer of action, if
> one seeks the performer of action and no performer of action
> be found anywhere, thereupon the goal of all fruit-obtaining is
> reached and also the final consummation itself.
> There being no other method whatsoever of obtaining the fruit,
> there is no need to fall under the sway of the dualities
> of accepting and rejecting, trusting and distrusting these
> teachings.

Hell, no. Try 'em. If they work for you well and good. If they don't, go somewhere where something does work for you and use that.

> Realization of the self-radiant and self-born wisdom, as the mani-
> festation of the tri-kaya in the self-cognizing mind, is the very
> fruit of attaining the perfect nirvana.

But you've got to get beyond your own little minds. You go to the end of your thinking and then jump off. See what it is! Try it! Couldn't do more than break both legs and your back.

THE EXPLANATION OF THE NAMES GIVEN TO THIS WISDOM

> This wisdom delivers one from the eternally transitory eight aims.
> Inasmuch as it does not fall under the sway of any extreme, it is
> called "the middle path."
> Being the essence of the vacuity of mind, it is called "the essence of
> the Buddhas."
> If the significance of these teachings were known by all beings,
> surpassingly excellent would it be.
> Therefore, these teachings are called "the means of attaining the
> other shore of wisdom."

Magnificent statements simply meaning Wake Up! Fall Awake! Weird. Very elegant names. A more vulgar way of saying it would be to fall awake and become aware of the reality of what you really are.

> To them who have passed away into nirvana, this mind is both
> beginningless and endless; therefore is it called "the Great

Symbol."

Inasmuch as this mind, by being known and by not being known,
becomes the foundation of all the joys of nirvana and of all the
sorrows of the sangsara, it is called "the all-foundation."

The impatient, ordinary person when dwelling in his fleshly body
calls this very clear wisdom "common intelligence."

He calls it "common intelligence," because you can look at someone else's
troubles and not have any empathy for the other fellow's position. You can
say, "That hasn't got anything to do with me and I'm clear of that. I'm
living in my own private world." You sure as hell are. But nevertheless, the
life that is sustaining you in this world is the life of the Oneness. A regular
person who has never looked for or seen any of these things, if that person
sees someone else suffering and doesn't have any empathy toward them,
he might say, "What the hell, that's their business." But anyone who has
dug the least bit into the *great perfection* of love, sensitiveness and empathy,
would immediately feel for that person and be sending him juice at another
level whether they knew it or not. "Common intelligence" and common
sense are synonymous. Common sense is one of the rarest things you'll
find, one of the most uncommon things.

Regardless of whatever elegant and varied names be given to this
wisdom as the result of thorough study, what wisdom other
than it, as here revealed, can one really desire?

To desire more than this wisdom is to be like one who seeks an
elephant by following its footprints when the elephant itself
has been found.

THE YOGA OF THE THATNESS

Quite impossible is it, even though one seek throughout the three
regions, to find the Buddha elsewhere than in the mind.

Although he that is ignorant of this may seek externally or outside
the mind to know himself, how is it possible to find oneself
when seeking others rather than oneself?

He that thus seeks to know himself is like a fool giving a
performance in the midst of a crowd and forgetting who

he is and then seeking everywhere to find himself.

This simile also applies to one's erring in other ways.

Unless one knows or sees the natural state of substances (or things) and recognizes the light in the mind, release from the sangsara is unattainable.

Unless one sees the Buddha in one's mind, nirvana is obscured.

When speaking of Buddha in this way, Buddha and Buddhi mean one and the same, that eternal spark within us.

Although the wisdom of nirvana and the ignorance of the sangsara illusorily appear to be two things, they cannot truly be differentiated.

It's all a Oneness in reality, all the different things are but the divisions of the lower levels of your consciousness, which you can understand if you come into awareness. We live in a world of duality and we have to learn to see through that duality. How can we see the Oneness if we're running one way or another. Whether it's money or energy, we say, "Oh, I gotta get to this, I gotta get to that." But can we look at it and see that it's just two sides of one thing. Look at it all from the standpoint of equilibrium of the middle path.

It is an error to conceive them otherwise than as one.

Erring and non-erring are, intrinsically, also a unity.

By not taking the mind to be naturally a duality, and allowing it, as the primordial consciousness, to abide in its own place, beings attain deliverance.

Or, as it says in the Good Book, "Be Still and Know I AM."

The error of doing otherwise than this arises not from Ignorance in the mind itself, but from not having sought to know the Thatness.

Seek within thine own self-illuminated, self-originated mind whence, firstly, all such concepts arise, secondly, where they exist, and lastly, whither they vanish.

This realization is likened to that of a crow which, although already in possession of a pond, flies off elsewhere to quench its thirst, and finding no other drinking-place returns to the one pond.

I would figure it's an awfully hip crow or else it got awful thirsty. We've got to do the same thing, get back inside ourselves and draw from that eternal fountain that never stops.

> Similarly, the radiance which emanates from the One Mind, by emanating from one's own mind, emancipates the mind.

LET GO! LET GO! LET GO and LET GOD!

> The One Mind, omniscient, vacuous, immaculate, eternally, the unobscured voidness, void of quality as the sky, self-originated wisdom, shining, clearly, imperishable, is Itself the Thatness.

That is the mind you're using, the ordinary mind is itself the One Mind. But you've got it caged in the little coop it's in because of what you've lived in former incarnations. Your subconscious part is telling you this is this and that is that. But right now, you're using that very thing that is the Oneness, that is the universality itself. Same as your breathing, you don't breathe yourself, you're in-breathed by the reality. You do it automatically. If you had to remember 21,600 times a day to take a breath, what else would you have any time to do? But you can't put your finger on it. You can't put it into a concept. Thatness! Is-ness! Be-ness! It's something that you have to experience. You have to function from there and BE THAT! You are That anyway, why not have the experience of doing it consciously? Thatness. Clear Light. Voidness. This is something that you have to experience by being it and you can only be it by going to that center inside yourself and being IT!

> The whole visible universe also symbolizes the One Mind.
> By knowing the all-consciousness in one's mind, one knows it to be as void of quality as the sky.
> Although the sky may be taken, provisionally as an illustration of the unpredicable Thatness, it is only symbolically so.
> Inasmuch as the vacuity of all visible things is to be recognized as merely analogous to the apparent vacuity of the sky, devoid of mind, content, and form, the knowing of the mind does not depend on the sky-symbol.
> Therefore, not straying from the path, remain in that very state of the voidness.

Voidness or Thatness or Clear Light or Awareness. These are all synonymous terms.

THE YOGIC SCIENCE OF MENTAL CONCEPTS

> The various doctrines are seen in accordance with one's own mental
> concepts.
> As a thing is viewed, so it appears.

In the ordinary language of the vulgaris that means everything depends on
how you look at it. Think it over. Is there anything that you know about
that doesn't depend on how you look at it? You can change your view if
you want to, no objection to it. You can look at something in a different
way, from a larger scope for the multitudinous sides of looking at it, and
then seeing it in its clearness for what it actually is . . . .

> To see things as a multiplicity, and so to cleave unto separateness, is
> to err.
> Now follows the yoga of knowing all mental concepts.
> The seeing of the radiance, which shines without being perceived, is
> Buddhahood.

As Hui-Neng said in his *Platform Sutra*, one minute you're a Buddha in
the way you're able to look at things, the next minute you're an ignorant
person. You touch all these things sometime in your life. Pay attention to
those which are important.

> Mistake not, by not controlling one's thoughts, one errs.
> By controlling and understanding the thought-process in one's
> mind, emancipation is attained automatically.

Of course, some people say that they can't control their minds. But you
can! It's up to you. The only thing is that it is difficult to control. If you've
hitched up your feelings and the baraka within you to a particular thing and
say, "That's the only thing." That type of a concept you find very difficult
to get rid of, but you can if you wish.

> In general, all things mentally perceived are concepts.
> The bodily forms in which the world of appearances is contained
> are also concepts of the mind.
> "The quintessence of the six classes of beings" is also a mental
> concept.
> "The happiness of gods in heaven-worlds and of men" is another
> mental concept.

"The three unhappy states of suffering," too, are concepts of the
   mind.
"Ignorance, miseries, and the five poisons" are, likewise, mental
   concepts.
"Self-originated divine wisdom" is also a concept of the mind.
"The full realization of the passing away into nirvana" is also a
   concept of mind.
"Misfortune caused by demons and evil spirits" is also a concept of
   mind.
"Gods and good fortune" are also concepts of mind. Likewise, the
   various "perfections" are mental concepts.
"Unconscious one-pointedness" is also a mental concept.
The colour of any objective thing is also a mental concept.
"The qualityless and formless" is also a mental concept.
"The One and the many in at-one-ment" is also a mental concept.

That's what we're doing here—mental conceptualizing. But maybe some
of it will sink in deep enough that it will get a little further.

"Existence and non-existence," as well as "non-created" are concepts
   of the mind.

When we think of something subjectively or we think of something ob-
jectively, neither one of them are pure mind. That which underlies it, that
makes it all possible, is pure mind. When we function in awareness, in that
case, awareness is not a thought, it's an attitude and a mood. Now the psychologist only deals with things of a conceptual nature, so the psychologist
as well as the others is still trapped.

The Realization and the Great Liberation

Nothing save mind is conceivable.

You can't conceive of anything that you don't have a picture of in your
mind.

Mind, when uninhibited, conceives all that comes into existence.
That which comes into existence is like the waves of an ocean.
The state of mind transcendent over all dualities brings liberation.

> It matters not what name may carelessly be applied to mind; truly
>   mind is one, and apart from mind there is naught else.
> That unique One Mind is foundationless and rootless.
> There is nothing else to be realized.
> The non-created is the non-visible.

The non-visible, or so-called non-material, from this level of consciousness we are functioning from now, but when you step into that other place, oh my, what an ecstasy there is!

> By knowing the invisible voidness and the Clear Light through
>   not seeing them separately—there being no multiplicity in
>   the voidness—one's own clear mind may be known, yet the
>   Thatness itself is not knowable.

Thatness is the awareness itself. When you're trying to grasp the awareness in your own mind, where does it come from? It slips away from you and it slides back. You can never grab it because that is what it is. Thatness, Clear Light, voidness—they're all speaking of the same thing. It's flipping the same concept at you under different headings, in the hope that you'll catch it. The Oneness is the underlying substratum of everything—physical, emotional, mental, everything—is of that Oneness, and we, in our clear state, when we get back home, will realize we Are. But we're drunk. We're doped up. We think the personality is us. But we still have our own place as one of the stars in the diadem of reality. When you try to see into that part of yourself, it's like awareness, and the more you try to grab it, it drops back further and further. You can't grab at it, because it just is. It's not a concept. It's awareness. It's reality. No! It's not knowledge as a concept. It must be something that you just realize you are, and you're functioning from that point.

> Mind is beyond nature, but is experienced in bodily forms.

And, oh man, do we get the experience.

> The realization of the One Mind constitutes the all-deliverance.
> Without mastery of the mental processes there can be no
>   realization.

It's a strange proposition, "mastery of the mental processes." If we don't wanna think about something, we can stop thinking about it. But we can't stop our minds from running and have it just clear. If we're tickled and real happy, that's one way out. Now sometimes, when you're in that great joy, drop the reason for the joy and enjoy the joy! That's the ananda state, man! All of your senses can be used to bring you to the reality, but you've got to be UP, you've got to be optimistic in your attitude. If you're in a morose or sad-sack condition you're never gonna expand anything. It's like if a man and a woman got together after they'd been in a refrigerator for awhile. I think it would take a long time for them to have anything happen. That's like the cold when you go into a pessimistic state. Keep it hot!

> Similarly, although sesamum seed is the source of oil, and milk the source of butter, not until the seed be pressed and the milk churned do the oil and butter appear.

I think we're getting a very strong pressing and churning in what's happening in the world today. In my own particular case, I think there's no oil left and the milk has been churned so long, it's not butter, it's cheese and I realize I'm a rat!

> Although sentient beings are of the Buddha essence itself, not until they realize this can they attain nirvana. Even a cowherd or an illiterate person may by realization attain Liberation.

Concluding Sections

> Though lacking in power of expression, the author has here made a faithful record of his own yogic experience.
> To one who has tasted honey, it is superfluous for those who have not tasted it to offer an explanation of its taste.

Suppose you were living in a place where there wasn't any large body of water and you wanted to learn how to swim and you had a library of books telling you how to swim, do you think you could swim after you got through reading the books? You'd have to get in the water. That's the trick with any of these teachings. Unless you use them, how do you know whether you know 'em or not. Oh, you could have just another soft tape in your computer there, but if you get too many tapes in your computer there ain't any room. You gotta throw some of 'em out! Sometimes I think if I could be a mental garbage man and I could collect all the loose stuff you got that's not worth a damn and leave the good stuff there, I'd carry it away and it'd be great. But I don't have that capacity.

> Not knowing the One Mind, even pundits go astray, despite their cleverness in expounding the many different doctrinal systems.

> To give ear to the reports of one who has neither approached nor seen the Buddha even for a moment is like harkening to flying rumors concerning a distant place one has never visited.

> Simultaneously with the knowing of the mind comes release from good and evil.

Just reality! Perfect energy. Perfect ecstasy. Perfect love.

> If the mind is not known, all practice of good and evil results in nothing more than heaven, or hell, or the sangsara.

Any kind of heaven that we're going to have when we get out of the vehicle is gonna be one we've conceived for ourselves and hell likewise. If we don't FALL AWAKE while we're here now and get so we can function at this level, we're gonna come back into incarnation again and again and when we see certain things that we ran into this time that we had trouble with, we'll have trouble again. Maybe your consciousness is a record of your former incarnations. But who just wants to come back again, when you can FALL AWAKE, and then come back knowing exactly who you are and what you wanna do and the work you wanna do in a lifetime? Wouldn't that be fabulous? Or else you can float off on Cloud 8, if you like. Huh? That is if you don't FALL AWAKE while you're here this time, and dig this for yourself. Of course, you'll get a wonderful heaven, the heaven you've pictured for yourself. But also, you'll get your delightful hell that you think you should be punished with. But if you FALL AWAKE and realize you're only having these heavens or hells because of the various incarnations you've gone through and haven't looked at and gotten rid of . . . . If you get rid of that software, WOW! There's no good or evil because if this is all a Oneness, anything evil or good, it's for the purpose of teaching lessons whether we realize it or not, and then having to pay off for them. Therefore, when you're beyond that, there is no good or evil. It just IS and YOU ARE and all you have to do is BE!

> As soon as one's mind is known to be of the wisdom of the voidness, concepts like good and evil karma cease to exist.

Of course! Where's the "evil karma?" It's in the causal body that we've collected over the years and once we've fallen awake to the reality, it isn't there. It's but a record that we keep as we go through until we can gain that consummate awareness.

> When as in the empty sky there seems to be, but is not, a fountain of water, so in the Voidness is neither good nor evil.
> When one's mind is thus known in its nakedness, this doctrine of seeing the mind naked, this self-liberation, is seen to be exceedingly profound.
> It is the vast deep.

> All hail! this is the knowing of the mind, the seeing of reality, self-liberation.
> For the sake of future generations who shall be born during the age of darkness, these essential aphorisms, necessarily brief and concise, herein set forth, were written down in accordance with Tantric teachings.
> Although taught during this present epoch, the text of them was hidden away amidst a cache of precious things.
> May this book be read by those blessed devotees of the future.

> These teachings, called "the knowing of the mind in its self-identifying, self-realizing, self-liberating reality," were formulated by Padma Sambhava, the spiritually-endowed teacher from Urgyan.

> May they not wane until the whole sangsara is emptied.

The Taksang monastery in Bhutan, built around the cave where Padma Sambhava meditated, on his way bringing Buddhism from India to Tibet

Young monks-in-training at the door of the Taksang monastery, 1988

Joe, down on the ground

Sam Lewis, in the 1950s

Annie Besant in 1925, when Joe met her

Evans-Wentz as a young man

Notes

1. Cyril Scott

Admired by Claude Debussy, Sir Edward Elgar, G.B. Shaw, and others, Cyril Scott (1879-1970) was not only a celebrated musical composer, he was also the author of numerous books of mystical philosophy, occult fiction, nutrition, and healing lore.

Crafted for seekers struggling in the western world of the 20th Century, Scott's *The Greater Awareness* expounded a holistic programme aimed at realization through the cultivation of love and awareness. In *Music: Its Secret Influence Throughout The Ages*, Scott articulated his views on how the works of masters such as Wagner, Beethoven, and Chopin affected the evolution of human consciousness.

One of Scott's piano pieces inspired Guin to work spiritually through the medium of music and she began holding Music Hour in the early 1950's. She always began the Thursday evening program by playing his work. In the following reminiscence, Guin tells of her introduction to Scott's music and later to the composer:

> It was in Los Angeles that I discovered Cyril Scott's "Lotus Land." Someone was playing it on the piano, and I was just walking down the street. I went up and knocked on the door. I asked what the number was and who wrote it. I went down to the book store and got a copy. It's been my theme song ever since.
>
> When we started the Music Hour which is going to have its thirty-fourth birthday in June someone asked if I had read the article by Cyril Scott in the *Psychic Observer*. I thought he had been dead for years. So I wrote to him in care of the *London Psychic Observer* and we corresponded up until the time he did pass on. That was a very happy time in my life and Joe's too. It was close to the time when we were getting married.

2. Evenings at the Lodge

In a tribute to Joe and Guin written for the Sufi Order's newspaper, *Hearts and Wings*, Suria Less captured the feel of the Miller's evenings at the lodge:

> Thursday Night Music Hour was a time when all were wel-

comed to participate, sharing their inspiration and talent. All were received there. There were times when the lodge reminded me of the Statue of Liberty—"Bring me your weary, your downtrodden, your hungry, your poor." People came for spiritual nourishment and were fed, in desperation for solace and were comforted, disheartened and were encouraged. A friend, Devi Lewis, reminded me that "Joe loved what he felt this country was really founded on—the freedom and opportunity, including material well-being, to pursue realization." He showed in what he did that the "pursuit of happiness" implied caring for the well-being of all. When Joe sang "God Bless America," it was truly a mystical experience. At Sunday night lodge meetings there was often a speaker. When the speaker was Joe, the place was inevitably packed. It was luminous and alive with the reality he so fervently wished to impart.

Hearts and Wings, Autumn 1992.

3. Guinevere Robinson Miller

The following is an excerpt from one of Guin's rare talks:

> I heard some beautiful music this afternoon. It reminded me of one of my music teachers who had studied at the Paris Conservatory. He had landed in Los Angeles at the same time I was living there, so I thought I would take a brush-up course. He told me that if I wanted to practice eight hours a day he could make me one of the ten best pianists living. But my baby was about the age of Joshua [four or five years old] at that time, so I didn't do it. And today I looked around at the audience and I thought, "Oh, this is much nicer, all my dear ones . . . ." I feel that choosing the human rather than the vain is the far better way. One of the lines from the Diamond Sutra comes to mind, "Who seeks me in form, who seeks me in sound, perverted are his footsteps upon the way . . . ." I just hope that in my choices I've made the right ones . . . .At that same time in Los Angeles, a voice coach wanted me to sing the soprano lead in the Messiah. But my first Capricorn [her first husband] had just gotten an opportunity for a better job in Portland. So, I again made the human choice instead of the vain one.

Guin was a disciple of the Master Jesus. As a child, she celebrated Easter sunrise up on her beloved Mount Tamalpais. She would cry, "Alleluia, He is Risen!" One of Guin's mentors was the Christian author and lecturer Walter C. Lanyon. She collected his many books, had one of his oil paintings hanging in her bedroom, and corresponded with him throughout the years. Lanyon's work is typified by this passage from *Laughter of God*:

> Deep in my soul, I heard the Laughter of God, ringing in silvery cadences through the timbers of my being, breaking the human bonds and limitations as a strong yet gentle wind in the forest sweeps aside the strands of cobweb. The hard, fast knots that I had tied slipped loose, and the snarls of beliefs broke free. The river of my human life, frozen by a thousand and one false ideas and teachings, broke joyously into expression and went bounding to the infinite sea of Life, to be lost and found at the same time . . . .

Among Guin's unique contributions to the culture of Theosophy were her "Songs to Live By," and "Thursday Night Music Hour," which she started several years before Joe even showed up on the scene. Once, when someone asked her to talk about music and its relationship to meditation and knowing oneself, Guin responded:

> I started formal lessons on my seventh birthday. But I had been at it for a long time before that. As far back as I can remember, music always pulled me out of anything. If my feelings were hurt or I was angry I would just go to the piano and do a few discords and pretty soon I'd get into harmony and I'd come out smiling. To me, there is just nothing like music.
>
> With music, if you just sit back and drink it in, you'll go beyond the mental and emotional levels and get off into Cosmic Consciousness and away from this minor stuff that we sometimes think of as ourselves. If you do that, you'll come back refreshed.
>
> All my life I could practically heal myself with music.

Guin's teachings resonated with a deep joy and acceptance:

> Don't worry, dear. Your rice is cooked from the beginning. Whatever happens is meant to happen. Everything works out if you just let it. You're never burdened with anything that you can't handle. Nothing is ever lost. No condemnations, no criticisms,

no comparisons and no complaints. If you can do that for just a week and really do it, you're a new person. We so easily fall back to just chit-chattering around. It's great to have a lot of fun and have everybody say, "Oh, be joyful . . . ." But you can be very joyful without being silly. And you can be very joyful while minding your own business. I'm sure that the Master Jesus wasn't minding other people's business, nor did he encourage his followers to do that.

4. Songs To Live By

Guin's compositions, "Songs To Live By," consisted of lyrics selected from the world's various sacred scriptures, such as "Never The Spirit" from *The Bhagavad Gita* (Sir Edwin Arnold rendition) and "Thus Shall Ye Think" from *The Diamond Sutra*; as well as a few poems, such as "Heart of My Heart" by Guin, "Only Through The Orchid Door" by Joe and "Ignore The Opinions of Others" by Richard Power. A recording of the Millers performing the whole song cycle was done by Sarmad Ocampo. The cycle has also been rendered as sheet music by W. Blake "BE" Derby.

5. S. S. Cohen

S. S. Cohen was a Jew from Baghdad who journeyed to India and ended up at Arunachala with Sri Ramana Maharshi. His correspondence with the Millers lasted from 1971 to 1975.

After receiving the newly published *Diamond Sutra and Sutra of Hui-Neng*, he wrote:

> I have seen Joe's introduction to the Sixth Patriarch and noted that he is an old hand in Buddhism. I am not new to it either. The Sixth Patriarch is pure Advaita—the Buddha-Nature, etc. But Bhagavan is modern and luminously direct. He is also full into all-round versatility.

After receiving a note in which Guin complained of too little time for introversion, he commiserated with her:

> Little "g." is wise to want at times to retire for "solitary

contemplation." There is no act under the sun which is more meritorious and more pleasing to the Self than the seeking of it. The very impulse to meditate is the result of its grace . . . .It is a reversal of the normal course of *sadhana* to abandon meditation in favor of work. After all, work is only the stepping stone—a "launching pad," if you like, to meditation. I am sure you know all this.

In one letter, he commended the Millers on their work, and humorously declined their offer to arrange a visit to America:

You are very right in taking up training the young. It requires special talents and patience and especially love in abundance. I do not mind being with you provided you send me with the aeroplane, specialists on heart, lungs, urology, and insomnia, with two nurses and operating equipment in case of emergency. Otherwise, do leave me where I am.

When the Millers remarked on how much they felt for the big photo of Ramana that hung in their living room, he playfully scolded them:

I am glad you see love in Bhagavan's eyes. It would be better if you saw the Self, the pure consciousness (Chit), the supreme knowledge, pure *jnana*. I am sure you are seeing your own love, for there is no one to be loved by Bhagavan. There is only the Self, the pure knowledge, as pure being.

6. Samuel Lewis

On January 15, 1971, Samuel Lewis departed the physical vehicle through which he had experienced this world for seventy-five years. Recognized as a Zen Roshi and a Sufi Murshid, Sam Lewis counted Papa Ramdas, Mother Krishnabai, Nyogen Senzaki, and Hazrat Inayat Khan among his teachers. Initiated into Buddhism, Vedanta, and Sufism, he traveled to Asia and the Middle East to study the great mystical traditions firsthand. He authored many books of mystical poetry, prophecy, and practices. Through divine inspiration, he originated the "Dances of Universal Peace" (Sufi dancing). These dances, with their simple movements, sacred mudras, and powerful mantras caught the imagination of the young in the Haight-

Ashbury of the late 1960's and early 1970's. Since then, Sam's dances have spread throughout the world. More importantly, however, Sam left behind a dedicated group of young people who are each working in their own way to bring an American strain of Sufism to flower.

Joe recalled Sam with great fondness:

I first met Sam in 1935. He had just come back into the Theosophical Society. He had been a member before he contacted Sufism. He'd always come back. After all, those principles held good in his life and they were the same principles expressed in Sufism.

I had just arrived here from the Midwest. I had worked in Chicago, then I went to Minneapolis. It was about thirty-five degrees below zero, and stayed that way for about a month. There was an ad in the paper, somebody was driving their car out to the coast and they would share the driving if someone wanted to go. After a month of that sub-zero weather, I said, "I'll go . . . ."

When I met Sam, he was rather abrupt. He was treating them, no doubt, the way they deserved to be treated around the lodge. "This isn't where it is; it's not in the books." He was giving it to them right then.

Sam was very flamboyant. People would say, "Well, if you know it, you won't say it, you'll be quiet." And Sam would say, "Most people who are quiet don't say anything because they don't know anything." So he put a switch on that, and there's a lot of truth in it. Particularly at that time, we had a lot of people in the T.S. who wouldn't answer you, if you asked them a question. They would just sit there calmly as if they were off in a different space. Sam couldn't condone that sort of thing, not even talking to people. He'd bring them right to now, right to what's happening!

Of course, he could be very much the other way. He could be very gentle. And the guy had a yiddish-kupf, he was no dummy. He always knew how to handle people. They thought he wasn't handling them right, or that he was too mean to them, or didn't understand them. But he did understand where they were at and was giving them a kick in the balls of their eyes to wake them up a little bit. I know because I had a guy come to the house in later years, saying, "Well look, can I be your disciple? Sam just kicked me out." I said, "Well, you idiot, go on back, if he loved you enough to kick you out, he really likes you. But if you don't bounce back, you haven't got anything on the ball. Just go down on the corner somewhere and forget about it. I don't take disciples anyhow." Well, he went back. I'm not going to tell you his name, but he got pretty important later.

Sam had definite views of where things were coming from and he never hesitated to express himself. He knew what he had, he was living it, so it meant something. Other people might have just been using conversational gambits to try to put an idea over from an intellectual side. But he felt and knew for sure where he was coming from, so he expressed himself and let the chippies fall where they may. That was how he lived, and he was a very disappointed man because people couldn't dig what he had to give. He had it, but they didn't seem to come for it.

But he grew to look at it from a broader view. When he started to have a bunch of kids around him, that's when the big transformation in Sam came about. Guin said, "He blossomed in the last three or four years of his life." A number of times I heard Sam say that his students made him what he was. In fact, that's something that a lot of people should remember if they are in a position of telling, talking, and teaching. He always said, "When I'm teaching them, they are teaching me at the same time, I'm getting as much or more from them than they are getting from me." This I don't believe is true for the simple reason that I believe he was giving from the depth of understanding and an open heart to them. But he was hearing different ideas and how people looked at things, and it gave him more expansion in the limited phase of the lower mind. And it was a wonderful attitude; not too many of them have that. Visit some of our swamis and you'll find they are talking down your neck, whether they are letting you say something or not.

Sam thought it was from the intellectual side that people would become aware of the New Age, but all the time that he was trying to do this, the effect of his heart, the effect of his coming into contact with his kids and his work with them was something else. He'd spend every dime he had and take a whole bunch of them somewhere. He gave them his heart, but he figured that the important thing was the intellectual side. But it wasn't the important thing. The important thing for the age that is coming is the heart, and he had so much of it that it spilled over on them and a lot of them caught it.

In the early days, he thought that the thing to do was get these authorities together and get them to say it, and then they could say it to the other intellectual ones and that would do it! But what really happened was that he gave so much of his heart to the people he did meet and that were close to him, that he planted seeds of light in them and they started to shine some. They were like the seeds in a pod that you get on broom. The seeds are very quiet until they reach the point of where they should be planted to grow more seeds, and then the thing snaps with a crack, and the seeds go in all directions.

Sam Lewis was a prolific and effusive correspondent. He wrote to friends and colleagues all over the world. During the mid-1960's, he vented his frustrations, honed his wit, and shared his discoveries in a series of letters to Joe and Guin. Sam was living down on Clementina Street. Joe and Guin were living up on Bush Street. The letters, kept in an old Pall Mall box in the Millers' cluttered office, offer a remarkable portrait of a great pioneer just as his life of searching, prayer, and struggle was finally beginning to yield results.

Thundering, Sam railed against his adversaries and articulated his own agenda:

> This morning I go to the Church of Universal Laughter where we study scriptures as dispassionately and as passionately as we study the sciences. You are expected to have had experience. We are not the phoney devotees who pray to the dead God for "Light." We are living vehicles for that Light, and sometimes the vehicles are quite young. This, of course, is impossible. Show me an old lady who will admit that the "lamb and lion shall lie down together, and a little child shall lead them." Nonsense. We aren't going to let any little child lead us. So we are a world of hypocrites and self-deceivers. We can't laugh, we can't let our light shine out, we can't do any of the things that the scriptures advocate, and we are all closed, each in himself or herself and are triply hypocrited by the nonsense about believing in the "brotherhood of man" and politely telling our neighbor to shut up. That is what we are.
>
> Well old Senzaki, whom I sometimes refer to as "noggin," left me seven forms of laughter and the old ladies can't take it away, nor the metaphysicians, nor the cults and you won't get it from Krishnamurti or Manly Hall either. Krishnamurti is a cloud of

perfume and Manly Hall an encyclopedia, but I haven't heard any stories about their auras.

I think I am the first man in the history of the world who has been initiated and ordained both as a Zen Master (by Seo) and as a Sufi teacher (chiefly by Sufi Barkat Ali in Pakistan), and who has sat not only "at the feet of the Master," real ones, not metaphysical symbols, and *with them*, which no self-respecting American is going to believe.

So I save all my notes, and when I am gone, they will be very valuable.

It is easy to teach with laughter, or with love, or with prajna, but it is impossible to reach closed minds, to impress rocks.

We have a war in Viet Nam because we want to teach Asians. We can't learn from them . . . .

Hearts unite and words and thoughts divide.

If you want to have fun, go to anybody, a person, a group, a whole audience and give them real teachings and they will reject you and eject you. Anybody who claims yoga knowledge is, of course, a pretender. So I am glad to be known as a pretender, an egoist, a fool. Yoga here depends on the social acceptability of the "teacher" and has nothing to do with "union-with-God."

Well, the young come. I ask them why. "Because you have been rejected. We only want to learn from those who have been rejected and ejected."

Somewhere along the way, Joe promised he would take care of Sam's disciples after Sam died. Several disciples, including Murshid Moineddin Karl Jablonski, Sam Lewis' designated spiritual successor, told of a fascinating exchange between the two friends during Sam's final days:

When Murshid S.A.M. was in the large ward at San Francisco General Hospital following his fall down the Mentorgarten stairs, a handful of Mureeds went to see how he was doing. While there, Murshid's long-time friend, Joe Miller walked in and, displaying an assurance lacking in the Mureeds, went directly to the bedside.

"Hey, Sam, it's your old pal Joe," he whispered.

"Huh, what?" Murshid reacted, opening his eyes indeterminately.

"It's your old pal Joe," he repeated. All of a sudden Murshid reached out and grabbed Joe's arm, yelling, "Take it!" Joe looked perplexed.

"TAKE IT!" Murshid yelled again, raising his voice and tightening his grip on the arm. Joe acted more dumbfounded.

"TAKE IT!!!" roared Murshid with finality, shaking Joe's arm clear to the socket.

"I'M TAKING IT . . . I'M TAKING IT!!!" Joe shouted with equal vigor. The ultimatum had been answered. Murshid lay back and was silent.

[Moineddin Jablonski, "Visiting Hours," *S.I.R.S. National Newsletter*, Vol. II, #3, September/October, 1987]

Of course, Joe insisted that Sam was just talking about a string of amber beads. Perhaps there was both an "ultimatum" and "a string of amber beads." Whatever happened between those two beings at that moment, Joe certainly kept his promise to "look after Sam's kids."

Joe delivered the eulogy at Sam's memorial service. The brief talk was preserved for posterity in the film *Sunseed, The Dawning of a New Consciousness* [Directed by Frederick Cohn, produced by Ralph Harper Silver and filmed in 1970 and '71, the documentary featured Pir Vilayat Khan, Yogi Bhajan, Swami Muktananda, Ram Dass, Swami Satchidananda, and Murshid Samuel Lewis among others.] I remember vividly seeing that film for the first time in a modern art museum screening room in N.Y.C., several years before I actually met Joe. The fierce white light of his countenance and the somber, yet wild depth in his voice on that occasion made a profound impression on me. **"You can get more stinking from thinking than you can from drinking," Joe bellowed, "but to FEEL is for REAL."**

After the shock of Sam's death wore off, in the mid-1970s, a period of great innovation and industry ensued, and continued on into the mid-1980s. One of the many ambitious endeavors undertaken was a "School of Sufi Studies," under the direction of Masheikh Wali Ali (a.k.a. Melvin Meyer, Sam Lewis' secretary.) The enterprise began in 1977 and was billed as "an organized attempt" to offer "an integrated course of study for the general public which can be pursued on a week-by-week basis."

During the School's brief but noble history, Joe taught a series of classes on Dr. W.Y. Evans-Wentz' *Tibetan Yoga and Secret Doctrine*. Every Tuesday for ten weeks, sitting on a sheepskin rug, below a painting of the Buddha, Joe discoursed on the dharma:

> Everybody wants space. The outer space is not as important

as guarding the inner space. By guarding it, I mean don't let it be obscured by your outer living. Whatever happens, I want you to know that nothing in the world can extinguish that inner spark of reality which each of you has. Because to complete the thing you have to do it here. The time when we retired to a mountain or to a monk's cell, that time is not for us who were born in America. I think that for those born in America who have a yearning for these teachings or for anything about IT, that those people have gone through those things in another lifetime, and what you need now is to bring that peace and joy into this life. You are trying to get to the point where you can continue what you were working on in your last lifetime.

In the early years of his Thursday Morning Walk, Joe would often host swarms of children from the Seed Centers (the group's experimental schools). Joe always carried a roll of quarters in his coat pocket. He delighted in placing a shiny coin in the small, upturned hand of each child. Joe was a member of the Seed Center's Advisory Board, and even contributed a short piece for their journal, *Sufi Wings*:

> The human seeds of light that come to us arrive carrying the fragrance of the glory in which they have resided. We on our side, in order to help nurture these seeds, must try to make them aware of their wings of light. Let them feel the warmth of the love within us that we share with them. Let them realize in an intimate way their membership in the fraternity of eternity. Make them aware of the responsibility of such membership. You really cannot tell them in words: a touch on the head, holding a hand, looking into the eyes, and maybe a word here and there, but mostly radiating from yourself the love that is their inheritance, so that the seeds of light within them may sprout and blossom, giving their fragrance to all.

7. Mahamudra

Concerning mahamudra, Joe referred to the scholarly translations of Garma C.C. Chang; specifically, *Teachings of Tibetan Yoga* which includes both "Essentials of Mahamudra" and "Song of Mahamudra," and *The Hundred Thousand Songs of Mahamudra*. In an appendix to the latter, Chang states: "the central teachings of mahamudra consists of two points: relaxation and effortlessness."

Tilopa's "Song of Mahamudra" describes this "practice of no-practice:"

Mahamudra is beyond all words
And symbols, but for you, Naropa,
Earnest and loyal, must this be said.

The void needs no reliance,
Mahamudra rests on nought.
Without making an effort,
But remaining loose and natural,
One can break the yoke
Thus gaining liberation.

If one sees nought when staring into space,
If with the mind one then observes the mind,
One destroys distinctions
And reaches Buddhahood.

Do nought with the body but relax,
Shut firm the mouth and silent remain,
Empty your mind and think of nought.
Like a hollow bamboo
Rest at ease your body.
Giving not nor taking,
Put your mind at rest.
Mahamudra is like a mind that clings to nought.
Thus practicing, in time, you will reach Buddhahood.

In mahamudra all one's sins are burned away.
In mahamudra one is released
From the prison of this world.
This is the dharma's supreme torch.
Those who disbelieve it
Are fools who ever wallow In misery and sorrow.

Teachings of Tibetan Yoga, pp. 25-27.

8. Madzub

In *The Inner Life*, Hazrat Inayat Khan tells of the Madzub's way:

He puts on the mask of innocence outwardly to such an extent that those who do not understand may easily consider him unbalanced, peculiar, or strange. He does not mind about it, for the reason that it is only his shield. If he were to admit before humanity the power that he has, thousands of people would go after him, and he would not have one moment to live his inner life. The enormous power that he possesses governs inwardly lands and countries, controlling them, and keeping them safe from disasters such as floods and plagues, and also wars; keeping harmony in the country or in the place where he lives; and all this is done by his silence, by his constant realization of the inner life. To a person who lacks deep insight he will seem a strange being. In the language of the East he is called a Madzub.

The Sufi Message, Vol. I, p.105.

9. Anger

The Kashmiri Shaivites understood this technique very well:

When an aspirant is under the domination of any strong emotion, he should disassociate his mind from the object of the emotion and concentrate deeply on the emotion itself, without either accepting or rejecting it. He should withdraw his mind from everything external and turn it within even as a tortoise withdraws it limbs within its shell on the occasion of a great danger. When he is thus intensely introverted, the passion becomes calmed like a charmed snake; all vikalpas are shed like leaves in autumn. Such abrupt introversion puts the aspirant in contact with the infinite spiritual energy surging within known as *spanda* and then he is filled with the bliss of divine consciousness—*cidananda*.

Vijnanabhairava, p. 92.

10. It Can Be Higher Than the Angels or Lower Than the Dogs in the Street

In his talks, Joe returns again and again to the theme of human love and sexual union. Irena Tweedie's teacher also emphasized the importance of the sex energy:

> Now I will tell you the secret of creation. Sex is the same in men and women; the ultimate moment of ecstasy in sexual relationship is the same in both. It may vary in intensity according to temperament and mood, but it is the same stuff. It is *ananda*—bliss, the only moment of real ananda on the physical plane in existence. It is the sweetest thing on earth.
>
> *Chasm of Fire*, p. 78.

11. Brahmacharya

Celibacy has been championed by some schools as a kind of religious and mystical ideal. Primarily, this bias has been advanced for two reasons. First, sexual passion is perhaps the most powerful attraction to the life of the body and therefore the cause of the greatest delusions and suffering. Second, occult lore suggests that sexual activity expends energy and leads to the loss of physical strength and spiritual magnetism.

Joe's approach, which he substantiated with the teachings of Sufism and Kashmir Shaivism, is to encourage seekers to embrace the whole of the physical world and understand the sexual dimension of love and life as a sacred opportunity.

Ramana Maharshi put a wonderful spin on the subject of celibacy:

What is the meaning of Brahmacharya?

Only enquiry into Brahman should be called brahmacharya.

Spiritual Teachings of Sri Ramana Maharshi, p. 33.

12. Moments of Ecstasy Outside of Meditation Practice

The Kashmir Shaivites also attempted to show the seeker the transcendent within the immanent:

> One can turn even a sensuous joy into a means of yoga. Joy of sexual intercourse is an example of *sparsa*—contact; joy at the sight of a friend is an example of the pleasure of *rupa*—visual perception; joy of delicious food is an example of *rasa*—taste; joy derived from a song is an example of the pleasure of *sabda*—sound.
>
> *Siva Sutras*, pp. 214-215.

13. Bhakti

The Sufi author, Fritjoh Schuon, offered some definitions of *bhakti*:

> For Shankara *bhakti* is what Moslems call *himmah*—spiritual elan. For Ramanuja it is continuity or perpetuity of contemplation. For Chaitanya it is limitless love.
>
> *Spiritual Perspectives and Human Facts*, p.157

The great 12th Century mystic Kabir sang:

> The *bhakti* path winds in a delicate way.
> On this path, there is no asking and no not asking.
> The ego simply disappears the moment you touch Him.
> The joy of looking for Him is so immense that you just dive in,
> And coast around like a fish in the water.
>
> *The Kabir Book*, p. 31.

In his study of the *Bhakti Sutras*, I.K. Taimni says,

> It may appear incredible that one can love with the greatest intensity what has no form, substance or sound, nothing to indicate its existence, but it is true and a matter of the most vivid and exquisite experience.
>
> *Self-Realization Through Love*, p. xiv.

14. Siva Sutras

Joe was thrilled when, in the late 1970s, a young friend handed him a translation of certain sacred texts from the tradition of the Kashmiri Shaivites. These works were compiled, translated and annotated by the eminent Indian Theosophist, Dr. Jaideva Singh. Joe had already been fascinated with the texts from an earlier translation by another Indian Theosophist, Dr I.K. Taimni.

The central work, *The Siva Sutras*, provides a systematic view of the whole framework of Kashmir Shaivism. Although many ancient scriptures offered Joe confirmation of his assertions concerning the direct method of dedicating one's incarnation to self-realization, few were as succinct, and clearly in tune with Joe's *jnani* side as *The Siva Sutras* and its companion volumes. In his commentary on the sutras, Dr. Singh elucidated several of Joe's major themes, for example:

> In the jiva or empirical individual, Reality or Siva or that divine transcendental Self is Light—Bliss that is ever shining within its glory but is hidden from our gaze on account of our thought-constructs. Reality is an eternal presence within ourselves. It is Siddha, an ever-present fact, not *sadhya*, not something to be brought into being by our efforts. It cannot be caught by the net of our thought-constructs, however clearly we cast it. The more we try to catch it, the more we try to grasp it, the more it recedes from us. We are prisoners of our own mind. Thought has to commit suicide in order to know our real Self, the Siva within ourselves. The dichotomizing activity of the mind has to cease. The wheel of imagination has to stop. The ghost of our discursive intellect has to be laid to rest, before we are allowed to realize our essential Self. When Vikalpa (conceptualization) ceases, the transcendental Self within us shines of itself. It is an experience in which the distinction of seer, seen, and sight is completely annulled. Thus when the mind neither accepts nor rejects any idea, its activity ceases and one abides in one's essential reality.
>
> *Siva Sutra*, pp. xxxiii-xxxiv.

15. Teachers

"Life has been my teacher," Joe said. "Guru" literally means truth. The stereotypical role of master and disciple is just one of several ways in which this process can take place, as Irena Tweedie's teacher remarked:

> The possible relationships between guru and disciples are: firstly, lover and Beloved—lovers in fact: this is mostly practised in tantra yoga; secondly, father and child; thirdly, master and obedient disciple; fourthly, friends.
>
> *Chasm of Fire*, p. 78.

Ramana Maharshi also handled this subject with care:

> I have never said that there is no need for a guru.
>
> All depends on what you call guru. He need not be in human form. Dattatreya had twenty-four gurus: the five elements—earth, water, etc., which means that every object in this world was his guru. Guru is absolutely necessary. The *Upanishads* say that none but a guru can take a man out of the jungle of intellect and sense-perceptions. So there must be a guru.
>
> I might have had a human guru at one time or other. But did I not sing hymns to Arunachala? What is a guru? Guru is God or the Self. First a man prays to God to fulfill his desires. A time comes when he will no more pray for the fulfillment of material desires but for God Himself. God then appears to him in some form or other, human or non-human, to guide him to Himself in answer to his prayer and according to his needs.
>
> *Guru Ramana*, pp. 67-68.

16. Spiritual Hierarchy

Ramana Maharshi gave a similarly evasive answer in regard to a question about "the spiritual government of the world:"

> Is there a spiritual hierarchy of all the original propounders of religions watching the spiritual welfare of humanity?
>
> It is only a surmise at best. One may accept such a hierarchy; another may not. But no one can gainsay the Self.
>
> *Reflections on Talks with Sri Ramana Maharshi*, p. 61.

One evening at the Lodge, during the late 1970's, Joe did refer to this somewhat hidden side of human incarnation. Whether he was teasing, hinting, or wondering aloud, I don't know, but this is what he said:

> Who knows how many if any—there may be some seated in this room—who are among the **Thirty-Six**? It is stated that the world couldn't run without the **Thirty-Six**. This is from the Jewish teachings. It is said that those thirty-six do not know what it is that they are here for, but that they are acting as channels to let flow through them what should be here to keep the world in balance. So who knows. There are similar things in the Sufi tradition. They are called certain names, they are not usually known. There are always so many in incarnation to keep the balance so that the Force will still be flowing through to humanity. Despite what they're doing at this intimate level, the Ultimate is pressing through.
>
> You might say, how could somebody be such a one and not know it? Well, he could be deaf or dumb. He could be a dummy or a cripple or a politician. No, no, I doubt that . . . . So you talk about a thousand in one chance, well, talk about the odds with all the billions of people living on the Earth. What are the odds that you're one of those carrying a lucky number? Maybe you've already come to another level, but you're being kept down at the point you are so THAT can flow through you. It's better than a billion to one, yet there are these ones . . . .

17. My Joy No Man Taketh From Me

Speaking to his disciples at the Last Supper, Jesus said,

> And ye now therefore have sorrow: but I will see you again,
> and your heart shall rejoice, and your joy no man taketh from you.
>
> *Holy Bible*, King James Version, John 16:22.

18. Heart

Ramana Maharshi elucidated this:

> God is said to reside in the heart in the same way as you
> are said to reside in your body. Yet the heart is not a place. Some
> place must be named as the dwelling of God for those who take
> their bodies for themselves and who comprehend only relative
> knowledge. The fact is neither God nor we occupy any space. We
> are bodiless and spaceless in deep sleep, yet in the waking state we
> appear to be the opposite. ATMAN or PARABRAHMAN is that
> from which the body is born, in which it lives and into which it
> finally resolves.
>
> *Guru Ramana*, p. 97.

19. Jnani

Ramana Maharshi offered a definition of the *jnani* way:

> *Jnana* is the annihilation of the mind in which it is made
> to assume the form of the Self through the constant practice of
> *dhyana*—concentration on the Reality, or enquiry—vichara. The ex-
> tinction of the mind is the state in which there is a cessation of all efforts.
> Those who are established in this state never swerve from their true state.
>
> *Spiritual Teachings of Sri Ramana Maharshi*, p. 22.

20. Just Be

Ramana Maharshi laid out the truth and the method of its realization rather bluntly:

> Your duty is TO BE and not to be this or that. I AM THAT I AM sums up the whole truth, the method is summarized in BE STILL.
>
> *Spiritual Teachings of Ramana Maharashi*, p. 75.

21. She Is the Creator

The passage which appears in the text is Coleman Barks' rendering of Book I, ll. 2432-2437 in Nicholson's *Mathnawi of Jalaluddin Rumi*.

Joe felt very strongly about the sacredness of the feminine principle, and the spiritual power of womanhood in the coming age. Toward the end of Joe's life, we talked about Mother Krishnabai. She had wholeheartedly, single-mindedly, taken the ageless way of the heart into utter surrender and fallen fully awake. She didn't need to redecorate the contents of her consciousness with other tapestries or mouthe different words. Joe concurred with Sam who had stated that Krishnabai was probably the "highest person on the planet" until her passing away. She went the way of the great *bhaktas*. No distinctions or differences are made among them. They don't differentiate between Allah and Ram, nor between man and woman. Kabir, Mirabai, Lalladevi, Bulle Shah—all were moths diving into the flame of selflessness.

What Joe saw coming in the New Age was the expansion of the heart, the deepening of compassion, and the refining of awareness. He saw the role of womankind emerging and growing as the understanding of the mystical life grew. This, he said, would happen naturally because the female vehicle is closer to the divine—"SHE IS THE CREATOR."

22. The Ancient Wisdom

First published in 1897, Annie Besant's *Ancient Wisdom* summarized the central Theosophical teachings into five "eternal verities," upon which the great world religions were established:

i. One eternal, infinite, incognizable real Existence.
ii. From THAT, the manifested God, unfolding from unity to duality, from duality to Trinity.
iii. From the manifested Trinity many spiritual Intelligences, guiding the cosmic order.
iv. Man, a reflection of the manifested God and therefore a Trinity fundamentally, his inner and real Self being eternal, one with the Self of the Universe.
v. His evolution by repeated incarnations, into which he is drawn by desire, and from which he is set free by knowledge and sacrifice, becoming divine in potency as he had ever been in latency.

The Ancient Wisdom, p. 5.

23. Krishnamurti

If true *messengers* are rare, then Jiddu Krishnamurti (1895-1987) was one of the rarest of the rare. For Krishnaji delivered two different, seemingly contradictory, certainly paradoxical messages to lost, toiling humanity.

His first dispensation began in 1909, at the age of thirteen, when C.W. Leadbeater and Annie Besant declared him to be the next World Teacher, the one destined to pave the way, the one who spoke as "the Coming Lord Maitreya." Leadbeater and Besant tutored and touted him, building the Order of the Eastern Star around him. At the apex of the commotion, many thousands flocked to huge barnfire meetings throughout the U.S. to hear from the young Krishnaji.

The T.S. seemed to be moving from its role as a society dedicated to the study of the "one ancient wisdom religion" which seeded all the world's great religions, to a new role as the foundation of a new world religion. Whether this burgeoning belief system would have been any more or less the faithful child of that "one ancient wisdom religion" is problematical. They started thinking they could do it better. Joe often quoted Krishnamurti's comment that as soon as someone has a good idea, the devil sidles up and whispers in his ear: "Let's organize it."

His second dispensation began in 1929, at the age of twenty-three, when Krishnaji disbanded the Order of the Eastern Star, renounced his role as "World Teacher" and walked away from the considerable wealth, comfortable estates and scented railroad cars that had been provided for him. He rejected his sponsors, the T.S., and the adoring throngs, to embrace the simple, solitary way outlined in his abdication declaration:

> I maintain that truth is a pathless path, and that you cannot approach it by any path whatsoever, by any religion, by any sect.
> Truth, being limitless, unconditioned, unapproachable by any path whatsoever, cannot be organized.
> I do not want followers. I mean this. If there are only five people who will listen, who will live, who have their faces turned towards eternity, it will be sufficient.
> I desire those who seek me to understand me to be free, not to follow me, not to make out of me a cage which will become a religion, a sect. Rather, they should be free from all fears.
>
> *Candles in the Sun*, p. 25.

24. Annie Besant

Long before she heard of Theosophy, Annie Besant (1847-1933) was famous (or infamous, depending on who you asked) throughout the English-speaking world. An Irish girl born in London, Annie got into an unhappy marriage to an Anglican minister, bore him two children, then got out. On her own again, she embarked upon a quest for justice as a champion of the downtrodden.

Annie Besant was the first woman who publicly advocated birth control and many other social and educational reforms. She was a freethinker, a materialist, and a diehard Fabian Socialist. She worked as a union organizer and strike leader. Her friend George Bernard Shaw dubbed her "the greatest woman orator of the century."

But when she met H.P. Blavatsky, Besant made yet another radical change in course. Or, as her biographer Nethercot wrote, "By 1893, she had completely cut loose from her rebellious and sensational past and had embarked upon an even more rebellious and sensational future." [*First Five Lives of Annie Besant*, p. 1.]

Asked to review H.P.B.'s *Secret Doctrine* for Stead's Pall Mall Gazette, Annie met Helena for the first time and told her editor: "I am immersed in

Madame B. If I perish in the attempt to review her, you must write on my tomb, 'She has gone to investigate *The Secret Doctrine* first hand.'" [*ibid.*, p. 268.]

Besant went on to succeed H.P.B. and her co-founder Colonel Olcott as International President of the T.S. and presided over perhaps the stormiest period in the outrageous history of the Society in her own controversial and dynamic way. [See Josephine Ransom's *Short History of the Theosophical Society*.]

During her time in India, she fought for "Home Rule" and actually served at one time as President of the Indian National Congress. Mahatma Ghandi admired her and considered her a friend.

25. W. Y. Evans-Wentz

Walter Yarling Evans-Wentz (1878-1963) was born in Trenton, New Jersey. He dropped out of high school. His desire was to become a journalist. He worked his way across the country in newspaper offices. He also had a nose for real estate and made some shrewd investments. Although he was a high school drop-out, he was accepted at Stanford University, but had to work with tutors to compensate for deficiencies in rudimentary skills.

After graduating from Stanford, he went on to study at Oxford and Rennes. He published his first book, *Fairy Faith In The Celtic Countries*, in 1911. His field of interest was religion and folklore. He spent six years traveling in the Mediterranean region, living in Egypt for three years where he studied early Gnostic traditions as well as ancient Pharaonic texts from Karnak.

In 1919, during a trek to Sikkim, he met his teacher and collaborator, Lama Kazi Dawasamdup. Described as an eccentric, otherworldly man with a penchant for drinking, this fascinating character also acted as translator for Alexandra David-Neel, author of *Magic and Mystery In Tibet*. Evans-Wentz was a bold pioneer whose concern wasn't simply scholarly. He was also a dharma explorer. This sense of purpose is expressed in his dedication for *Tibetan Yoga and Secret Doctrine*, "To them that shall succeed me in the quest on Earth."

In the late 1950's, Joe wrote an essay on the Clear Light which Evans-Wentz edited for him. Although the short piece was never published, it gave Joe an opportunity to formulate some ideas. In his edit, Evans-Wentz struck a paragraph of Joe's and contributed one of his own as a substitute. Evans-Wentz' contribution was one of Joe's treasures, and he recited it at the conclusion of his Lenten readings of *The Great Liberation*.

The Clear Light is the source of light that lighteth everyone of humankind that cometh into the world. It is the radiance of cosmic consciousness. Yogins realize it while still in the fleshly body and all humankind glimpse it at the moment of death. It is the light of the Buddha, the Christ, and all masters of life. And to the devotee in whom it shines unimpededly, it is the guru and the deliverer.

The following passage from Joe's initial draft is the one Evans-Wentz cut out:

Now let's talk about that nasty stuff that everyone likes to hear about, you know—SEX. This is the point from which we are all jet-propelled. With it you can reach the stars, or beat yourself to pieces against the rocks. Or, if you are very fortunate, enjoy "unendurable pleasure, indefinitely prolonged." Did you ever see a picture of an alligator trainer subduing, or as they say, hypnotizing an alligator? If you have not, here is what the trainer does—he strokes the belly of the alligator and the alligator becomes very satisfied. Have you ever had your belly stroked? If you have not, have it done, and I am sure you will find in some respects we are all related to alligators. It arouses feelings of warmth and desire. It does not create a possessive desire but a warm glow so that everything looks and feels rosy. Remember always your seeds or roots in physical incarnation are in SEX. Friction or movement create heat and fire. Stillness leaves one cold. Oh, I'm not through writing about SEX, I'm just starting.

In later years, Joe was fond of asking, **"What does everyone really want? I'll tell you—unendurable pleasure indefinitely prolonged. Yeah, and you can have it too, if you're willing to BE IT and LET IT FLOW AS UNSELFISH LOVE FROM INSIDE OF YOU. Try it, you may like it."**

26. Be Still, Be Very Still

Ramana Maharshi:

> And what does stillness mean? It means "destroy yourself," because every name and form is the cause of trouble. "I-I" is the Self. "I am this" is the ego. When the "I" is kept up as the "I" only, it is the Self. When it flies off at a tangent and says "I" am this or that, "I" am such and such, it is the ego.

> *Spiritual Teachings of Sri Ramana Maharshi*, pp. 75-76.

Bibliography

Ramana Maharshi and Related Sources

Baleskar, Ramesh S., *Pointers from Sri Nisargadatta Maharaj*, Acorn Press [Durham, N. C., 1982].

Cohen, S.S., *Reflections on Talks with Sri Ramana Maharshi*, T.N. Venkataraman [Tiruvannamalai, 1971].

——, *Advaitic Sadhana*, Motilal Banarsidas [Delhi, 1975].

——, *Guru Ramana*, T.N. Venkataraman [Tiruvannamalai, 1967].

——, *Forty Verses on Reality by Ramana Maharshi*, Watkins [London, 1978].

Frydman, Maurice and Dikshit, Sudakkar, *I Am That: Talks with Sri Nisargadatta*, Acorn Press [Durham, N. C., 1982].

Godman, David, *Be As You Are: Teachings of Sri Ramana Maharshi*, Arkana [London and Boston, 1985].

Maharshi, Sri Ramana, *Spiritual Teachings of Sri Ramana Maharshi*, Shambhala [Boulder and London, 1972].

Bhakti Yoga

Kabir, *The Kabir Book*, tr. Robert Bly, Beacon [Boston, 1977].

Krishnabai, Mother, *Guru's Grace*, Anandashram [Kerala, 1964].

Lalla, *Naked Song*, tr. Coleman Barks, Maypop [Athens, Ga., 1992].

Taimni, I.K., *Self-Realization Through Love*, Theosophical Publishing House [Adyar, 1975].

Buddhism

Chang, Garma C.C., *The Hundred Thousand Songs of Milarepa*, University Books [New York, 1962].

——, *Teachings of Tibetan Yoga*, University Books [New York, 1963].

Evans-Wentz, W.Y., *Tibet's Great Yogi Milarepa*, Oxford University Press [London, 1951].

——, *Tibetan Yoga and Secret Doctrine*, Oxford University Press [London, 1958].

——, *Tibetan Book of the Dead*, Oxford University Press [London, 1957].

——, *Tibetan Book of the Great Liberation*, Oxford University Press [London, 1954].

Gilbert, Don, *The Upside Down Circle*, Blue Dolphin Publishing [Nevada City, Ca., 1988].

——, *Jellyfish Bones*, Blue Dolphin Publishing, 1980.

Luk, Charles, *Vimalakirti Nirdesa Sutra*, Shambalah, Clear Light Series [Boulder and London, 1972].

Price, A.F. and Mou-Lam, Wong, *The Diamond Sutra and the Sutra of Hui-Neng*, Shambhala [Boulder and London, 1969].

Rinpoche, Thrangu, *Buddha Nature: Ten Teachings on the Uttara Tantra Shastra*, Rangjung Yeshe Publications [Kathmandu, Nepal, 1988].

Winkler, Ken, *Pilgrim of Clear Light, the Biography of Dr. Walter Y. Evans-Wentz*, Dawn Fire [Berkeley, California, 1982].

Kashmir Shaivism

Singh, Jaideva, *Siva Sutras*, Motilal Banarsidass [Delhi, 1979].

——, *Pratyabhijnahrdayam*, Motilal Banarsidass [Delhi, 1963].

——, *Vijnanabhairava*, Motilal Banarsidass [Delhi, 1979].

——, *Spanda-Karikas*, Motilal Banarsidass [Delhi, 1980].

Judeo-Christian Tradition

Buber, Martin, *Tales of the Hasidim: Early Masters*, Schocken [New York, 1968].

Eckhardt, Meister, *Sermons and Treatises, Vols. I-II*, tr./ed. M.O. Walshe, Watkins [London, 1981].

Lanyon, Walter C., *The Laughter of God*, L.N. Fowler and Co. [London, n.d.].

Sufism

Lewis, Samuel L., *This Is the New Age in Person*, Omen Press [Tucson, 1972].

——, *In the Garden*, Harmony Books and Lama Foundation [New York and San Cristobal, N.M., 1975].

——, *Introduction to Spiritual Brotherhood: Science, Mysticism and the New Age*, Sufi Islamia/Prophecy Publications [San Francisco, 1981].

——, *Jerusalem Trilogy*, Prophecy Pressworks [Novato, Ca., 1975].

——, *Talks of an American Sufi: Love, Sex, Relationships and Other Selections*, Sufi Islamia/Prophecy Publications [San Francisco, 1981].

Khan, Hazrat Inayat, *The Sufi Message*, Volumes I-XII, Barrie and Rackliff [London, 1960].

Khan, Pir Vilayat, *The Call of the Dervish*, Omega Publications [New Lebanon, New York, 1981].

Nurbaksh, Dr. Javad, *What the Sufis Say*, Khaniqahi-Nimatullahi Publications [New York, 1980].

Rumi, Jelaluddin, *Open Secret*, trs. Coleman Barks and John Moyne, Threshold [Putney, Vt., 1984].

——, *We Are Three*, tr. Coleman Barks, Maypop [Athens, Georgia, 1987].

——, *Delicious Laughter*, tr. Coleman Barks, Maypop [Athens, Georgia, 1990].

Schoun, Fritjhof, *Spiritual Perspectives and Human Facts*, Perennial Books [London, 1969].

Tweedie, Irena, *Chasm of Fire*, Element Books [Tisbury, Wiltshire, 1979].

Theosophy

Besant, Annie, *The Ancient Wisdom*, Theosophical Publishing House [Adyar, 1918].

Blavatsky, H.P., *The Secret Doctrine*, Adyar Edition, Theosophical Publishing House [Madras, 1971].

——, *Voice of the Silence*, Theosophical University Press [Pasadena, 1971].

Bowen, Robert, *Madame Blavatsky on How to Study Theosophy*, Theosophical Publishing House [Madras, 1960].

Collins, Mabel, *Light on the Path*, Theosophical Publishing House [Madras, 1911].

——, *When the Sun Moves Northward*, Theosophical Press [Wheaton, Ill.,1941].

——, *Idyll of the White Lotus*, Theosophical Publishing House [Madras, 1933].

Krishnamurti, J., *At the Feet of the Masters*, Rajput Press [Chicago, 1911].

——, *First and Last Freedom*, Harper and Row [New York, 1975].

Lutyens, Lady Emily, *Candles in the Sun*, Rupert Davis [London, 1950].

Nethercot, Arthur, *First Five Lives of Annie Besant*, University of Chicago Press [Chicago, 1960].

Ransom, Josephine, *Short History of the Theosophical Society*, Theosophical Publishing House [Madras, 1938].

Scott, Cyril, *The Greater Awareness*, Samuel Weiser [York Beach Me., 1981].

Taoism

Wei, Henry, *Guiding Light of Lao-Tzu*, Quest Books [Wheaton, Ill., 1982].

Cleary, Thomas, *The Essential Tao*, Harper [San Francisco, 1992].

Photo Credits

Front Cover
Joe laughing: Nirtana S. Bluestein

Back Cover
Joe and Guin on Mt. Shasta: Malika Anderson

Page 33
Joe, Guin, and Ramana: Unknown
Joe in the circle: Unknown
Joe, Guin, and Lama Chime: Shabda Kahn

Page 34
Guin: Carolyn Roos Malleck
Guin with her son, Leighton Mackenzie: Unknown
Joe rapping: Carolyn Roos Malleck

Page 40
Guin: Nirtana S. Bluestein

Page 127
Guin and Malika: Allaudin Mathieu

Page 131
Sam Lewis: Unknown

Page 137
Joe: Allaudin Mathieu

Page 138
On the walk: Sharon Haas
In front of the lodge: Claudia Singer

Page 139

Joe, Guin, and Lamala (Lama Dudjom Dorje): Nirtana S. Bluestein

Joe, Guin, Guin's brother Lance Robinson, and Richard Power: Chris Chater

Page 140

Two photos of Joe and Guin leaning against a tree: Allaudin Mathieu

Page 141

Wonder Bread: Carolyn Roos Malleck

Page 169

Scenes from the walk: Matin Mize

Page 170

Joe, the student prince: God knows

Joe, the doe-eyed gangster: Sussman, Chicago

Page 200

Taksang Monastery: Ministry of Tourism, Bhutan

Young monks in training at the door of Taksang Monastary: Jim Moore

Page 201

Joe with children: Unknown

Joe with Bob and Mary on the walk: Matin Mize

Page 202

Sam Lewis in the 1950's: Unknown

Dr. W.Y. Evans-Wentz: Unknown

Annie Besant: Unknown

Page 228

Joe hugging Devi Mathieu: Allaudin Mathieu

JOSEPH DUSTIN MILLER
January 20, 1904 — August 19, 1992

GUINEVERE ROBINSON MILLER
April 19, 1904 — November 4, 1992

Somewhere, somehow, in this country,
we're going to have something of our own soil,
that we can put into people's hands,
and into their hearts,
so they won't have to pay toll to anybody.

In the Long Tradition of Spiritual Rascals . . .

Joe is in the long tradition of spiritual rascals who are very, very useful
teachers; they come along now and then, and walk through the park
with magnificent love and acerbity.

—*Ram Dass*

What would the great beings of antiquity be like if they came back to the
world today. They might chew tobacco—Joe did. They might sing
in vaudeville—Joe did. They definitely would love—fiercely and
without judgment—as Joe did. And by their presence, they would
awaken. Certainly, Joe did that, indiscriminately, for all those who
would let him.

—*Shahabuddin David Less*

Joe Miller said "Wisdom can't be taught, it has to be caught." Richard
Power's *Great Song* is a major league catcher's mitt!

—*Stephanie Salter, San Francisco Examiner*

Joe Miller never claimed to be a teacher, yet he influenced the lives of
many people by planting the seeds of wisdom. For Joe, study-
periods were a time for mutual sharing—never didactic, often
humorous, always supportive. Joe helped his fellow seekers avoid
the pitfalls and keep love and laughter in their hearts.

—*Don Gilbert, Zen Master (Cho Ke Order)*

Joe Miller is one of the greatest people you have had in your country. He
left no descendant. You don't need more. Everybody who has tried
to leave a descendant ends up with a foundation. What happens
with a foundation? It collapses. Right. When you are in the present
moment, you understand what I mean.

—*Reshad Feild*

Joe Miller taught a uniquely American approach to realization, free from the cultural trappings which surround so many mystical traditions. His words, edited by his long-time friend Richard Power, are a burst of loud, passionate light and love; a primer on merging with divine consciousness through common sense, humor, and love informed by intelligence.

—Vasheest Phillip Davenport, founder of the Sami Mahal Sufi Center

Joe Miller was one of those rare individuals who could sing themselves through life, and by singing inspire others with the beauty, wonder, and excitement of incarnation. The songs Joe sang were both steeped in wisdom and enchanting in their simplicity. He and Guin made us all richer and the world a better place for their passage through it.

—Joy Mills, former National President of The Theosophical Society In America

Joe and Guin Miller lived in a simple way; not distracted by the material illusions of this existence, but demonstrating the contentment arising from their deep realization. They were a living example and inspiration for all practitioners.

—Lama Dudjom Dorje, representative of H.H. Gyalwa Karmapa, (Karma Kagyu Lineage)

Homage to a great emissary of the Clear Light! May all who glimpse this book find the high road within the heart. May the Love that Joe and Guin lived flow through us all like a river, and kindness walk the Earth again, unveiled.

—Zuleikha

Joe Miller's existence proved, and continues to prove, that pristine sanctity springs up unexpectedly in every culture, including so-called modern western culture, bearing all the transformative, elevating force, humor, and freedom that it has always borne. Joe Miller is the heart of the planet, the heart of spiritual wholeness, our own most intimate heart.

—Lex Hixon (Sheikh Nur Al-Jerrahi)